John Philipps Emslie

New Canterbury Tales

John Philipps Emslie

New Canterbury Tales

ISBN/EAN: 9783337074807

Printed in Europe, USA, Canada, Australia, Japan

Cover: Foto ©ninafisch / pixelio.de

More available books at **www.hansebooks.com**

NEW CANTERBURY TALES.

New Canterbury Tales,

BY

John Philipps Emslie

London:
GRIFFITH, FARRAN, OKEDEN, & WELSH,
Saint Paul's Churchyard.

ALL RIGHTS RESERVED.

	PAGE
THE PROLOGUE	1
THE SQUIRE'S TALE	8
INTERLUDE	23
THE ANTIQUARY'S TALE	33
PROLOGUE TO THE SPINSTER'S TALE	71
THE SPINSTER'S TALE	76
PROLOGUE TO THE WORKING-MAN'S TALE	89
THE WORKING-MAN'S TALE	93
THE PLOUGHMAN'S TALE	100
PROLOGUE TO THE AUTHOR'S TALE	115
THE AUTHOR'S TALE	118
EPILOGUE	133

NEW CANTERBURY TALES.

The Prologue.

RMA virumque cano. Very good.
A good beginning, so I've under-
  stood,
Is half the battle. So? Well, the
  first three
Words that I've chosen (you'll with
  this agree)
Are very good; and so are the next two;
Then the first line is very good. Is't true
That half the battle's fought? Is't possible?
What of the other half? Wait; time will tell.
A better half, for quantity, no doubt;
A worse for other things some may give out
Opinion, as they read page after page.
But here some little thoughts my mind engage.
How can a half be better or be worse,
Larger or smaller, whether prose or verse,
Art, science, commerce, houses, goods, or gold,
Than fellow half, since we've been ever told
That halves are equal? Yet we often see,
In their contents, such inequality,

That we begin to ask what halves may mean,
Since they in ever-changing forms are seen.
Take half of eight; twice two, or four times one,
And see how different halves in form may run,
When equal area's not of equal length,
While equal size may have unequal strength;
A whole mob's wisdom often will not reach
To half of what one learned sage can teach;
When two take halves in sharing wisdom, it
Not follows they take equal shares of wit;
And, two wits being equal, oft we find
Their gifts unequal; so wills Fortune blind;
And then, again—stop, lest my brain, o'erwrought,
Should find it's travelled farther than it ought.

Thus thought I, as, in fancy, once I went
Along that pleasant road in fertile Kent
That's known as Watling Street. I rode a horse
That lightly carried me along the course;
Though you'll say I did ne'er on horseback act;
But this is fancy; don't forget that fact.
My head, with gloomy lumbering thought opprest,
So heavy grew, it drooped upon my breast;
It had, with heavier thought, dropped at my feet,
And thought no more; 'tis thus extremes do meet.
When, on a sudden, a sharp clattering sound
Of hoofs disturbed my thought, and, looking round,
I saw, swift coming onward, and with force,
A heavier man than I, a heavier horse

Than mine he rode, and on, with slackened rein,
With noise, and cloud of dust, they came amain.
Foreshortened, terrible they seemed to view,
As, nearing swift, they large and larger grew.
They puzzled me; theirs looked like hostile act;
I might, or might not, soon be fierce attacked,
So keenly watched to see what was his aim,
If in mere sport, or, as a foe, he came.
Oh! trying moments; me he soon would reach;
Still on he charged, came near, came close; then, each,
Soon as he plainly could the other see,
In voice, deep bass affecting, growled, "'Tis he!"
But who the "he" was, I'll not here avouch,
It was, perhaps, like children's game of touch,
Each, thinking he was right, could have no doubt
But that the other was the one who's "out."
And then he drew his sword from out its sheath,
That is, his tongue from 'neath his closèd teeth,
And with his weapon fiercely laid about
With snarl, with sneer, with snort, with snub, with shout.

Oh! what discourse. It seemed that love and hate
Not one from other knew in his debate.
Great love of fellow-creatures he'd profess,
You might have thought him pure unselfishness,
Till against others fiercely he'd declaim,
Denounce their cruelty, their backward aim,
From his so diverse, and then bid you see
Their greatest crime, with him to disagree.

"I'm a Progressionist!" he roared, "that's straight;
I am for clearing every five-barred gate
That's closed, for there is property in that;
All property is robbery, that's flat;
Where did the owners get it? Come, tell me;
And we will give it back; to whom? You'll see;
And you are one of those who think folks should
Keep whatsoe'er they've earned; yes, and you would
Let every man be free; but I have said,
And will maintain——"
      Why did he turn his head?
And why did I turn mine? We hard did stare;
A something mystic seemed to be in th' air;
Struck dumb, we looked back, but, upon the road,
For some half-mile, no living being showed,
Neither upon our ears came any sound
Which should have causèd either to look round;
And, as the less is conquered by the great,
Common surprise ended our warm debate;
Each with raised brows did at the other look,
Then wheeling round, his way in silence took
As far apart as width of road allowed,
While swift through each mind strangest thoughts would
  crowd.
Not ten yards had we gone, when, in our rear,
Quite close, we both of us at once did hear
The click of horses' hoofs upon the ground,
And buzz of chat, and laughter's lightsome sound;
At once we turned, and then saw such a bright
Procession of fair folks, it cheered our sight,

Although our minds it somewhat did affright ;
Quaint in its form, rich coloured was each dress,
As in some Harleian or Royal MS.
Though with dismay we hard at them did stare ;
How was it they so suddenly came there ?
Had they sprung up from earth ?   Or fallen from
    high ?
Or formed in air, like cloud in summer sky ?
We could not tell, appalled we held our breath,
Sat like two statues, motionless as death.
Next our dismay to pleasure did give place,
For very prepossessing was each face,
And gave us confidence, and chased our fears ;
These were old friends of some five hundred years ;
The Knight, the Squire, the Prioress, and who
But Chaucer's self, and all the Pilgrims too.
Then, as aside to give them room drew we,
Out spake the Host, " What men now may ye be ?"
" Sir Host," said I, "we ben two moderne menne
Which riden on o waie, although that whenne
We viewen life, we rouken on eche side
The road of life, as up on lond so wide
Ye han so———."   " Peace, no more I thee beseech,
But speak thy nineteenth-century strange speech
Just as thou list ; for it we understand
As well as anybody in the land.
Beyond our day, when Time scarce fifty years
Had flown, we spoke some words in Lydgate's ears ;
When Time had flown o'er two more centuries
Then with John Dryden we could talk with ease ;

And next we told our tales in Pope's smooth rhyme;
Why, my dear fellow, we'll talk to all Time,
Wherever English, just 'as she is spoke,'
Shall be pathetic, or shall make a joke.
　"Now, you are in our fellowship to-day,
And, if you like to tell, why say your say
About this day's adventure.　Now attend,
You'll hear again, but this time brought to end,
At least some kind of end, the young Squire's tale.
Tell what you hear.　Fancy's inconstant gale
Is softly blowing, and it sways you so
That it seems fact, while facts as fancies show.
Others have told of what their fancy threw
About our words, and, truly, so may you."
"Sir Host," said I, "with friendship you abound;
But you and yours, where English folks are found,
Are always friends, and of old standing too."
"Sir," said the Host, "my thanks I offer you;
But, let us pass compliments; we will address
Ourselves, without delay, to business.
I wait for two, now riding down a lane,
A brother and his sister, soon they'll gain
The main road, and with us shall spend the day,
For each, in turn, will have something to say."

Soon as the Host had ceased to speak, the two,
Of whom he had just spoken, came in view.
Surprised they were, and thought to ride away,
But Host's frank words of greeting made them stay.

The new-found pilgrim was of portly size,
With white hair, full voice, and with kindly eyes,
Which spoke his nature, for he kindness showed
To all he met upon life's varied road.
His sister, younger, many years had been
One of the race of maids, and now, I ween,
Wishing that her we might in good light see,
Tried, with success, agreeable to be.

"Now, lordings," said the Host, "'tis time that we
Begin our sports. The gallant young Squire, he
Will go o'er some old ground, then tread on new,
And his strange horse of brass again we'll view.
And now, once more, tell us your tale, young Squire,
And add to it." "I'll do as you require,"
Replied he; then with his tale he sped,
In some such words as it may here be read.

Now some, perhaps, may say, "Pooh! Such absurd
Tale from a Chaucer-hero ne'er was heard."
Others, "Well, we will let such effort pass,
'Tis very plain that brass begetteth brass."
But what I ruled before I'll re-enact,
That this is fancy; don't forget that fact.
In fancy we o'er everything can fly,
The strange, the commonplace, the low, the high,
And 'twas in such a flight this tale I heard,
So, if I have not given it word for word
Just as the Squyer told it, be it read
As 'twere some dream that's half rememberèd.

The Squire's Tale.

ONG since there lived, in Tartary afar,
A king who was with Russia e'er at war,
And, in his wars, fell many a doughty man;
This noble king was namèd Cambynskan.
A mighty monarch, blest with everything
In mind, thought, power, worthy of a king.
For he was hardy, wise, of courage bold,
Maintained the laws he'd sworn he would uphold,

Was true of speech, benign, and honourable,
Rich, powerful, and eke in conduct stable.
He had two sons, by Elthetha, his wife,
Of whom the elder was named Algarsyfe,
The other son was named Camballo ;
A daughter had this worthy king also,
His youngest child, and Canace was named,
Through all the kingdom for her beauty famed.

It was this monarch's wont as, in each year,
His birthday came, to keep, with regal cheer,
At Bakchi Serai, in his palace fair,
High festival, and, on that day, to share
Joy social with his nobles. I would fain
Speak of the twentieth birthday in his reign.
The hall was crowded with the proud and great,
With nobles, courtiers, ministers of state,
Ambassadors, and princes from afar,
And mail-clad guards, his valiant men of war ;
Where swarthy faces and dark gleaming eyes
Glowed duskily 'mid splendour of rich dyes,
Of gorgeous colours, of pale hues, of gold,
Of glittering gems, of silk, and stately fold,
And tight-bound sash, and ornament so free,
And coloured stripe; that there no rest could be
For eye bewildered in the maze of rare
Embroidery, feathers, jewels, textures fair,
Thinking each wondrous, ever passing on
From others, which, in turn, its gaze had won.

And there the great, the royal Cambynskan,
The mightiest, where mighty was each man,
Sat high in state, and wore his diadem,
And kingly robes, adorned with many a gem.

Pleasure flew lightly o'er the scene, for when
From distant places fellow-countrymen,
Each with his local thought, together meet,
Then comes good fellowship with converse sweet.
And, when the talk was loud and mirth was great,
And harpers 'gan, with music delicate,
To play those airs the nation knew so well,
And silent were the guests as worked the spell,
Of music which brought thoughts of country's
    fame,
In at the hall-door suddenly there came
A stranger knight, riding a horse of brass,
In his right hand he held a looking-glass,
A golden ring upon his thumb he wore,
And by his side a naked sword he bore.
And on he rode, up to the king's high board,
Whilst, in the hall, not one dared speak a word,
Awed by the knight and glittering horse of brass,
As it, with stately step, did onward pass
Among the guests, who sat all motionless,
Silent, and filled with strange uneasiness.
Then, as they gazed, if there had been one thought
Of terror, to mere wonder soon 'twas wrought.
The strange knight carried such a noble air;
As, clad in glittering armour rich and rare,

With bare head nor by helm nor turban bound,
His manly face well seen by all around,
When he the king, and queen, and lords, with mien
Of grace saluted, none had ever seen
Such courtesy so deep, such observance
Of tone of voice or play of countenance,
Of manner evidence of lofty mind,
In bravest knight, most polished or most kind.

He said, "O king, for ever live. I bring
From my liege lord, Arabia's great king,
His royal wish that every blessing great
May light on you and on your regal state.
 "In honour of your feast, he sends, by me,
This horse of brass that easily and free,
With turning of a pin, will move or stay,
And high in air will soar, or downward stray
To any place you wish, how far soe'er
It be, and in one day 'twill bring you there.
 "This mirror, too, that I hold in my hand,
Is such, that you at once may understand,
By looking on its face, when there shall be
Any mischance or drear adversity
Unto yourself, your friends, your realm also,
And, at a glance, who is your friend or foe.
And any lady fair therein may view
Her lover's heart, and know if it be true.
So sendeth he this ring and glass I bear,
To Lady Canace, your daughter fair.

"This ring possesseth such a charm, when she
Wears it, whatever kind of bird there be
That speaks to her, she'll know his meaning plain,
And in his language answer him again.
And every herb that works for mortal good
She'll know, and where it grows in field or wood.

"This naked sword, that hangeth by my side,
Such power hath, that it will straight divide
The strongest armour, whensoe'er it strike,
However lightly; there is not its like,
For, whosoe'er is wounded with its blow,
But touch the wound with the sword's flat, and, lo!
However wide or deep may be the wound,
'Twill close at once, and leave the flesh all sound."

Graciously spake the king, the fair princess
Smiled her sweet thanks, while pleasure's sighs express
Applause half uttered by the nobles all.
The knight bowed gracefully, and from the hall
Rode to the courtyard, and did there alight
From the strange brazen steed that shone so bright.
Then, by a page, was to his chamber ta'en,
And his ringed armour there aside hath lain.
Then (to the hall returned) before the king,
To Canace he doth present the ring
And eke the mirror; and the wondrous sword
Gives to the king, sitting at festive board.
Then, seated at the noble feast, the knight
Joined pleasantly in conversation bright;

And, after supper, with the king did pass
Into the courtyard, where the horse of brass
Stood firm as rooted rock; he showed the king
The way to start the horse, to make him spring
Aloft from earth, how, next, to bring him low,
Then, how to make him pace, or swift or slow;
The way to make him disappear from sight;
And, as he showed this, it had vanished quite.

First blankly stared, then faintly laughed, the king,
Not yet quite used to things astonishing.
Then to the hall returnèd with the knight,
And talked and feasted till near morning light,
Where all were merry and with joy elate.
And here I'll leave them in this happy state.

Now speak I of fair Canace. She heard,
Early one morn, a poor distressèd bird
Tell her a tale of sorrow and of pain,
And, as it grieved, she answered it again,
Nor thought it strange she understood each note
It uttered, and could answer it by rote.
The virtue of the magic ring she wore
Made that familiar which was strange before;
But now 'twas easy, as 'tis e'er when we
Have confidence of perfect mastery.
Sweet sympathy was in her face so fair,
Giving fresh beauty to her beauty rare.
Compassion warm lit up her tearful eye,
Cast on the moaning bird that droopèd nigh.

It was a falcon, grieved and pained at heart;
To Canace she plained, the bitter smart,
Her true love's loss; for hence her lord had flown,
And of some other bird more fond had grown;
Her he had left whom once so well he loved,
Who loved him with a love by trials unmoved.
But, though his falsehood was to her so great,
Him she still loved, nor cared for other mate;
Forsaken now, of dearest love bereft,
No happiness on earth for her was left.
Oft she, with both her wings, deals furious blows
Upon her sides, when forth the warm blood flows,
Till, faint and weak with woe and loss of blood,
The maiden, pitying its anguished mood,
Took the poor bird, and for it wrought a mew,
By her bedside, covered with velvet blue,
And mixed an ointment for its wounded side
From gathered herbs which the kind fields provide.
And, in the end, the bird her love did gain,
Not till Camballo journeys strange had ta'en.

Fierce Algarsyfe, when this sad tale he heard,
Vowed he would seek the caitiff perjured bird,
And bring him to his heart-struck mate again.
Yet, think not Algarsyfe felt any pain
For the poor falcon. He was fond of fight;
War and adventure were to him delight;
But, as peace reignèd new, this task would find
Passing employment for his active mind.

THE SQUIRE'S TALE.

His sister bade him to her chamber come,
And she would ask her bird where her love's home
Might be, and, as for them the nearest way
Unto her room across the courtyard lay,
They crossed the courtyard as the stranger knight
Came forth, and, instant on their startled sight,
(As if void air had formed in solid mass)
Came into view the magic horse of brass.
Then Algarsyfe, impulsive, at one bound,
Leaped on its back, and turned the pin around.
"Oh! Stay!" shrieked Canace in blank despair
As horse and rider all at once in air
Went up, and flew with quick ascending flight,
With growing speed swift gaining greater height.
"Oh! Brother, go not—father!—mother!—stay!"
She shrieked, and felt that she could run away,
Yet paused, with doubts distracted, while her cries
Rang through the hall, and filled with dire surprise
King, queen, and courtiers; in confusion they
Start from the table, to the yard away
Hurry, affrighted. "See!" the princess screamed,
And pointed upward, while unto her seemed
So terrible the sight, she turned her round
And, with her head half drooping toward the ground,
Her one hand covered o'er each closed eye,
The other pointed upward to the sky.
They looked in terror. "Stay," the king and queen
Together cried, "my son, my son, oh! bring
Not sorrow to us by this headstrong flight."
He now, so high, was almost out of sight;

Soon but a spot, next as a mere speck showed,
Then lost to sight in intervening cloud,
And, as the cloud passed, he no more was seen.
When, overwhelmed with grief, the king and queen
Unto the palace turned with hearts of lead,
And for Algarsyfe mourned, as he were dead.

Soon as Algarsyfe rose above the ground,
He tried, in vain, to make the steed turn round.
He could not manage it in any way,
And swift each moment farther he did stray
From mother earth. All void of fear was he,
Yet wished himself from this adventure free.
He was quite baffled, who so well could ride.
Across great Gobi's arid desert wide
Once had he ridden, all from end to end,
On his brave steed, which seemed as some good friend,
So well he'd carried him, so well had made
Response to bridle touch or varying shade
Of voice. But this brute vainly he tried to guide,
Some stubborn sprite in him must, sure, abide.

Still up he rose. He saw the fields below,
So sweetly green, 'mid streams that gently flow,
Round them, the desert with its parched white sands,
And, on its edge, the purple distant lands,
The mountains rugged, many a dreary peak,
And shade-filled valley, where with mortals speak
The jin, the div, those spirits with frames of fire,
Who dare to human wisdom ne'er aspire,

Yet much are feared, because of their great power,
Which may wreck mortal in unguarded hour.
"Oh! prophet, keep me from Kâf's rocks," he cried,
Then to the pin in horse's head applied
Himself once more, turned it another way
By chance, and, swift though he had risen that day,
As swift he downward sank; now how to steer
The magic brute he knew; each moment near
And nearer came the earth, then rose the dim
Thought 'twas some foreign land unknown to him.
The air was softer, brighter far the green,
And nature all luxuriant was seen.
The arid desert, dreary steppe, away
How far he knew not. Here might peris stay
He thought, on seeing rich and massive trees,
And streams, and gardens; sweetly blew the breeze;
Whilst some fair sight came into nearer view
Each moment; cornfields of a golden hue,
Dark fruitful vineyards, villages, walled towns,
And minarets whose domes the crescent crowns.
He heard strange shouts from many a startled crowd
Who, looking up, in wonder, cried aloud;
He saw them hurrying on to where he might
(As they thought) come, but, hidden from their sight,
The horse flew down, amid four lofty walls,
Upon a lawn; around were waterfalls,
Fountains, and arbours, beds of beauteous flowers.
Dismounting, swiftly then Algarsyfe scours
Each nearer path, unmoved by beauty here.
This was but scene of some adventure near,

For every place, to him, was but a stage
Where deeds, not thoughts, a warrior should engage.

And, as he saw a stately palace, fine
In its proportions, beauteous in each line
Of its wrought marble, straight for it he made,
And soon within its open porch had strayed ;
There paused, in hope that some one might appear,
Or friend or foe he cared not, lost to fear ;
Then, striding on, entered a dome-topped room,
Cool in deep shade that was devoid of gloom,
For the strong sunlight, wandering, here would fall
In warm reflected light on floor and wall,
On marble white, on deep carved pillar's head,
On porphyry dark with veins of rich soft red,
On the tiled dado's mellow whitish hue
With flowered scrolls of mystic green and blue,
Where oft some large embossèd tile would show
A Korân-text amid the colours' glow,
'Neath where, through openings of carved lattice-screen,
In little spots the hot blue sky was seen.

He heard a step, and, soon, a princess bright
Came forth, then started, terrified at sight
Of Algarsyfe, and tremblingly stood still ;
Sharp fear had ta'en away from her her will ;
She could nor move nor speak, and feared the worst,
Since such strange man had in her chamber burst.
" I," said Algarsyfe, " whose this palace is,
Some faithful true believer's surely 'tis ;

This text I know, though it I cannot read."
Blankly the princess stared, a time of need
It was for her, who'd in her life ne'er heard
Of any foreign language half a word.
At last, with modest prayer, " Oh! tell," said she,
" Strange being, if from earth or air you be ;
Or if—— " Algarsyfe laughed. Now, when a boy,
He had been made (and this did him annoy,
Who'd be nought but a warrior) to learn
The Persian tongue, his father could discern
That 'twould be well to know his neighbour's speech,
That false translators might not him o'erreach.
Dully the fighter learned, soon left behind
His learning, but it now came to his mind.
He spoke, and loudly did the princess laugh ;
Her courage came, hearing that paragraph
Of Persian, ungrammatical and bad,
And ill pronounced. It almost made him mad
To hear a woman laugh so at so great
A being as he thought himself ; his hate
Began to rise, for such as he require
That all who them behold must them admire.
He frowned, and with rebuke began to speak,
Fear seized the princess, once more paled her cheek,
When, through the open doorway, came a band
Of maidens, who one moment made a stand,
Shocked at the sight of Algarsyfe, a man
Alone with their princess ; then swiftly ran
Unto her side. " Your parents come," they said,
And then the king, and queen, and courtiers made

An unexpected entry. "We have heard,"
Thus spoke the king, "and it hath been averred
By one we doubt not, that there have been seen
A man and horse the sky and earth between,
And both descending to the palace ground.
Ha! He is here; him we alone have found!"
Then, to Algarsyfe speaking, " Is it true
That, from the sky descending, in the view
Of my astonished subjects, you have come
Here on a horse of brass? Why, how could roam
Such steed, if such there be?" "Well, look, for there
He is," said Algarsyfe, "in the open air."
Swiftly flew all to where, upon the grass,
Stood, firm as rock, the stolid horse of brass.
"Now," said Algarsyfe, "here, before your eyes,
I'll do a feat will cause you great surprise.
I gain and keep all things by strength of fist."
He, sudden, seized the princess by the wrist,
Then with both arms he lifted her, and ran,
While, stupefied, astonished, not one man
Moved, but, as sense returned, quick closed around
Algarsyfe, as he did on horseback bound,
And turned the pin, and up they flew in air,
And, when some thirty feet aloft they were,
He turned the pin again another way,
Which caused the horse aloft in air to stay
Like some poised bird. "Aha!" he gleeful cried,
"A Tartar I, I scorn to woo a bride,
But snatch, and ride away, and she is mine.
Who'd to a woman's fickle will incline?

Who with his sword can beat brave men, he ne'er
For women, but as spoil, should ever care.
Who by swords live, know none have aught by right,
Save what they keep by strength, or gain in fight.
She's mine. But, come ye on, I'll fight you all,
Or one, or many, who, at glory's call,
Will meet me in the lists. But first, my bride
Shall to my home be ta'en, whate'er betide;
This is our Tartan practice. You may send
Your heralds to our court, I will defend
My right unto the bride that I have won;
She must the worthiest love. I am that one."

Oft did the archers draw their arrows out,
Yet, vacillating, paused, in painful doubt;
They might the princess hit, or, should they gall
The prince who held her, she, perhaps, might fall.
The spearmen threatened, women, courtiers raved,
And the affrighted parents vainly craved
Of Algarsyfe the boon, their daughter dear
To spare, nor cause them shed the bitter tear
Which, flown from racking sorrow, endless woe,
Felt for a loved lost daughter, e'er must flow;
Conjured him by Mohammed, but in vain;
And offered gifts and honours, wealth and gain.
"Send when you please! Prince Algarsyfe, re-
 nowned,
At Bakchi Serai Palace will be found.
Aha! Ahoigh!" He turned the pin aright,
Swift rose the steed, and soon was out of sight

Of parents terrified, and crazed with grief
To which no mortal aid could bring relief.

Here pause I for awhile. Some day I'll tell
Of the adventures which to all befel.
How the princess her courage did regain,
And so befooled Algarsyfe, with a chain
Of love she bound him. How she got away
Soon after they arrivèd at Serai,
And on the horse sprang, and away did fly,
(For she had wheedled from him, when on high,
The secret, how to work it) and returned
Home, and now found her heart with strange love burned
For prince so bold, who, sure, as brave a man
As Roostem was; thus love with her began.
I'll tell, too, of the war Algarsyfe waged
Against the Persians, of the fights that raged
In fields and lists, how victory him did bless,
And of his marriage with the fair princess;
Of Camballo, as well as Algarsyfe,
And who it was had Canace to wife;
And of the stranger knight, who brought the ring,
Mirror, and brazen horse, to Tartary's king.
I'll tell of ins and outs, of ups and downs,
Of joys and sorrows, and of smiles and frowns,
Of love, hate, peace, war, dark despair, bright hope,
All things with which we mortals have to cope,
Which were endured by each true knight and dame,
And how all safely through their trials came.
But, lordings, ask not now for more, I pray,
For other tales have to be told to-day.

Enterlude.

"IN truth, Squyer, thou hast thee
    well y-quit,"
Quoth the Franklin, "and
    well I praise thy wit."
Quoth the Progressionist,
    "You praise it, eh?
Well, yes, I s'pose so, every-
    thing you say
Some one will back up, some one will applaud."
"Well," said the Host, "if you desire the laud
Of this good company, tell thou a tale,
And, to your face, to praise you we'll not fail."
"Oh! good; hear, hear!" we all of us did cry,
And then, in silence, waited his reply.

"Is this a time," he asked, "when great events,
Falling in places smooth, make heavy dents
Which 'twill be hard to mend; I ask, at such
A time as this, when none can do too much
To help the cause of progress; yes, I ask,
Again, if all should not join in the task

Of pushing progress forward, and not waste
The time on telling tales which please the taste,
Or may amuse, but which, for earnest men,
Are quite unfit? And now, for progress, when——"
"Stay," said the Host, "that's not our business;
We meet to tell tales, nothing more nor less,
At least to-day, and other things proclaimed
Here are but hindrances, though progress named."

Said the Progressionist, "You little know
Of things, now making such a glorious show,
We men of progress mean to shape anew,
And give to them the world in novel view.
Old prejudices we shall sweep away.
As those who turn the night into the day
Can show that daylight's no necessity,
Nor needful, as folks fancied it to be,
So we'll show things, that from of old have been
Thought right, may altogether wrong be seen.
"Now, property has duties, we've been told,
As well as rights, and, might I be so bold
(For I would speak with deference unto
Wise men's remarks) I'd say you'll find this true;
As human-nature yields to well-pressed suits
You will be certain to get some recruits
If you'll hold up some banner time enough,
No matter for what cause; or flimsy stuff,
Or real wisdom. Hang out that red flag,
The tongue, and long enough but let it wag

'Bout property's great duties, but its rights
Put in the background, until misled wights
Deny, as this you o'er and o'er recall,
That property has any rights at all,
And agitate to seize whate'er they can,
Whate'er belongeth to some other man,
To Church, to landlord, city guild, whate'er
Belongs to others, they'd place 'neath the care
Of whom? Of those whose ideas will be lost
Unless they're carried out at others' cost.
And, could we gain all these, who then would know
Unto what farther seizures we might go?
   "Why don't we do it then, you ask me, eh?
Well, there are just a few things in our way.
Could we thrust these aside, we then should be
Able to do great wonders; what, you'd see.
   " Look at that time, two centuries afar,
When men designing caused a civil war,
They plunged the country into fearful strife,
They seized their King, and robbed him of his life,
Then they abolishèd the House of Lords,
The House of Commons, too, soon afterwards;
Victorious rebels put the Lords to rout,
A troop of soldiers threw the Commons out,
And the whole nation then was truly free
From civil and religious liberty.
A general victorious ruled the land
With boundless power whose might none could withstand,
Whoever served the Church in danger ran,
For state-made creeds were thrust on every man.

"Now if, to-day, we could the same thing do,
And crush the Lords, we'd crush the Commons too.
No doubt we could, for, as you plainly see,
This is th' experience of history.
The House of Lords is representative
Of many qualities which aye shall live
Long as humanity has reverence
For dignity above mere things of sense;
For sons of mighty ancestors are there,
Many who've risen by their merits rare,
And represent religion, law, and arms,
And service to the state; no false alarms
Can them displace, not votes they represent,
Nor numbers, in a changing parliament;
But, with them, study, culture, intellect,
To making laws their talents will direct.
But all of this we want to set aside.

"I'll tell you what we did one summer-tide.
The Lords once passed a bill meant to protect
The poor men's daughters from that loathsome sect
Who'd steal from them their virtue. What d'ye think?
The People's House (we call it) did not shrink
This measure to reject, and, afterwards,
It had a quarrel with the House of Lords,
And we, who wished that House we might destroy,
Thought now our time had come; ah! with what joy
We spoke to working-men, and talked of right,
But kept that Crim. Law Bill out of their sight;
Those very working-men, whose daughters most
The rake's and procuress's toils accost,

Urged on by us, full oft declaimed with glee
'Gainst those who would their benefactors be.
  "Now I have shown to you a glorious cause,
All shall be sacrificed to brand-new laws.
I think my plans you all can understand,
So now, my friends, let's grasp you by the hand,
And all be in one boat." "Right," said the Host.
"Now tell your tale, let no more time be lost."
"Lost?" said the other. "Come now, that's not just.
No; I won't tell a tale, but, if I must
Tell something, here it is, here's something light.
  "I was out with some chaps the other night,
Some o' the right sort, too, and no mistake,
Together met, and first my old friend spake;
'Twas Jimmy Link; he occupied the chair,
And made a speech, that all the men did stare
As well as listen, for it was so good;
Its arguments were clear, well understood;
With statements false 'twas exquisitely graced,
Whilst fallacies most cleverly were placed.
Ended his opening speech, 'twas not too long,
He upon Charcoal called to sing a song;
'Twas fiery Charcoal, whom none dared oppose,
Whose fury in his face so plainly shows,
And everybody thought that Charcoal's song
Would like his native self be, fierce and strong;
But no, he sang about a flowery vale,
And how he met fair Lucy in the dale;
A song of sweetness and the month of June,
Which he sang loud, with voice all out of tune,

Like donkey's bray, while, scowling, he looked round
To see if in the meeting might be found
One who by word or deed, shrug, hint, or whim,
Dared show the slightest disrespect to him;
No, though to find such feeling he did try,
Not one, as round he glanced, would meet his eye.
Then Giddy Giddy Gout essayed a dance,
And, as he up and down did leap and prance,
He gained applause; this gave him confidence,
And round he spun with energy intense,
Whereat a mighty cheer burst from the crowd,
With shrieking laughter, vigorous and loud;
And Gout, delighted, spun him round about,
All heedless of their half-sarcastic shout;
He took their laughter for a pure delight
In his performance: was he wrong or right?
Then Georgey Porgey told the doleful tale
Of how his gallantries did always fail
To please the fair sex, for he made them cry
When he some well-meant kisses fain would try.
And Pott o' Bere told how, one Sat'day night,
He lost his wife; his joy and his delight!
And how he sought her, how, and where, and when,
While tears rolled down the cheeks of these strong men.
But, when he told them how that her he found
In midst of a huge crowd that stood around,
They burst out laughing; this did him surprise;
The moment previous tears were in their eyes.

At his surprise they laughed with might and main;
He frowned and scowled; their laughter strength did
  gain;
This maddened him, and he, with closèd paw,
Landed a good one on his neighbour's jaw;
Then, in an instant, both were on their feet,
And, with coats off, a waltz they danced so neat,
Where partners held not hands, but thrust them out,
With doubled fist, each at the other's snout.
But Charcoal rose, and said, 'That blow was foul.'
Another rose; another; soon a howl
Of angry portent from each throat arose,
While fists were doubled to back cons and pros,
Each shouting loud for what he thought was right;
And soon there was a jolly good free fight."

"Well," said the Host, "is this the kind of thing
That you'd amid harmonious people bring?
Come, come now, friend, and tell to us a tale."
"What!" said Progressionist, "can any fail
When such a cause——?" "A tale, for order's sake,
'Tis now your turn; we all must give and take."
"Eh! what?" he roared, "well, this is cool, I vow;
To whom do you say this, I'd like to know?
What! give and take? That's good, sure as I live;
We take, but no Progressionists e'er give.
Don't you judge us by ordinary laws,
We're too great to abide by such, because——
But I have told why, and, if to my way
You won't submit, I'll here no longer stay."

He clapped his spurs unto his horse's side,
And swiftly back along the road did ride
Up rising ground, and, as his head was reared
Against the sky, another head appeared,
Coming the other way; they met atop
Of the ascent, and there awhile did stop,
Where the Progressionist, with waving hand,
And wild air-beating, hard to understand,
Talked on, though we heard not a word he said,
Until, at length, the other shook his head,
And forward rode, while the Progressionist
Downward fast galloped, and from sight was missed.

Then onward came the other, and, when near
Unto us, much surprised he did appear,
And held aloof; but said the Host, "We're friends,
And you for th' absentee shall make amends."
"What!" said the other, "was he one of you?
Stand off: for some think anything will do
For such as we. I'm a plain Working Man,
Whom some folks would into their plots trepan.
But no; I keep my course, and hold my own,
And mind my business, and when has flown
Into our midst some evil-omened bird
Who us 'gainst richer brethren would have stirred,
I turn round to such men, and I say, 'No;
If you can better do than they can, show
The way, but at your own expense; take not
What's theirs to do it, or a most hard lot

'Twill be for them and us at once, when you
Have theirs and ours within your grasp.'" "Too
 true;"
Said then the Host, "most plainly it appears
Such live by setting brethren by the ears."
"Well," said the Workman, "many, many such
I've seen, and, by your leave, 'tis not too much
To say of them, themselves they worship so,
That, at the last, they think the world would go
Much better than it does, if only they
Could force and jostle all into their way."

"Now," said the Host, "that all is peace again,
I think that I might ask for some round plain
Unvarnished tale ; not of that fearful brood
Would harrow up the soul and freeze the blood."
Then to our old white-headed friend he spake,
"Sir, would you tell an old tale for the sake
Of the old times, which you, no doubt, esteem,
For you're an Antiquary, as I deem ?"
"Sir Host," the other said, "you honour me.
To tell a tale to such a company
I should be pleased ; but, sir, my time has flown
In poring over many a parchment brown,
In studying abbeys, churches, ruined walls,
Half-timber houses, old baronial halls,
Weapons and armour ; oft I've taken turns
'Mid barrows, celts, and cinerary urns,
Pondered o'er bronzes, flints, and ancient chests,
Stained windows, monuments, and palimpsests.

But, sir, you've asked me, I'll do what I can.
An ancient tale, writ by a modern man,
Was never finished, but a friend of mine
Took it and added to it his design.
I'll tell it, if within your scheme 'twill fall."
"Good," said the Host, "now listen, lordings all."

The Antiquary's Tale.

WHILOM in England
lived a gallant lord,
All wise in counsel,
valiant with his sword,
In nature noble, honour
free from stain,
Roland de Vaux, the
Lord of Tryermaine.

His castle strong, as near or far 'twas seen,
Showed as a dark grey mass in landscape green;
Its sullen moat reflecting forms of power
Of keep, and thick-built wall, and jutting tower,
And loopholes black, hinting at men unseen,
There hidden, ready with their arrows keen.
In scene so fair how grim the castle seemed,
By death inhabited, one might have deemed
From outer view, but, ah! within its walls,
Its guardrooms, chambers, armouries, kitchens, halls,
With life were busy, with the constant stir
Of many a servant, warrior, officer.
Here lived Lord Roland, here he kept his state,
In wealth and power, a baron proud and great,

Restlessly grieving for the loss of two
Whom he had loved with heart's affection true;
His gentle, loving wife, whom death had ta'en,
And friend he'd parted with in quarrel vain.
With him Squire Richard dwelt, his only son,
And how, in warfare fierce, his spurs he won,
I'll tell.

Well, when my tale begins, young Richard, he
Was just at that age when the young men see
"The vision of the world and all the glory that would
 be,"
As says the poet. Happy they who gain
That which their young ambition strove t' obtain;
But sad for those who through life struggling go,
And ne'er gain what they seek with toil and woe.
Young Richard dreamed of honour and of love,
Each would by turns, then would together, move
His mind, but not his heart, him seemèd there
That much was wanting; many a maiden fair
Was beauteous to his eye, and oft would move
Him for some days, e'en weeks, to thoughts of love.
But thoughts would fly, and leave no love behind,
So oft he deemed, this pondering in his mind,
He scarce should worthy be to be a knight,
For ancient hero loved some lady bright,
And, for her sake, slew giants, dragons, foes
In countless numbers, and, though he'd oppose
Himself to any enemy that came,
'Twould honour be, not love, would raise his fame.

He was not cold, nor him did fair ones scorn,
He was a favourite, handsome, young, well-born.
And, as life's vision opened on his view,
And yearning nature called for partner true
To share his heart, and with that heart be one,
And none responded, then his mind would run
On thought of who'd be best 'mong those he knew,
And, far in front of others, there stood two ;
Whom would he wed, if he must choose a bride,
Beauty sans gold, or plain with lands so wide?

Over this matter, too, Lord Roland thought.
He wished his son to marry, but ne'er sought
To urge him marry wealth, yet thought 'twas quite
As well to have broad lands as beauty bright ;
Better, perhaps ; at Roland's time of life
Men have new views of how to choose a wife.
How much he wished his son might love as he
Had loved his lady ; happy then 'twould be.
But Richard seemed not to such love inclined
As may be seen when two hearts are entwined
In one. So, if in love he ne'er might be,
His father hoped he'd marry prudently.

One morn, Squire Richard, careless what to do,
Diversion seek, or resolution true
To form, went from the castle, full of thought
Shifting, uncertain, and his steps soon brought
Him to the bridle-path, and, as he strode
Across its track, he saw where onward rode

A band of men bound for the Holy War,
The cross sewn on their dress. Ah! If afar
In paynim land, he thought, 'twere well to fight
And with such leader, that renownèd knight,
Prince Edward, Evesham's victor, what renown
He there might gain. Soon was the thought nor flown,
Nor yet retained; it dwelt with him, and fled,
And oft returned, as oft he turned his head,
Each time to see how they e'er smaller grew,
Till, far away, they disappeared from view.

All things diverted him, none gave him rest,
Yet no loved image moved an anxious breast,
For his was calm, and every thought was free,
Some pleasure came in all that he could see.
He saw the oxen draw the clumsy plow,
The hooded forester with grim cross-bow,
Leaves sprouting glittered 'gainst the pale spring sky,
He heard, o'erhead, the lark's sweet melody.
He in the wild land struck, he climbed a hill,
And then, for miles, strayed through a valley, till,
Passing a jutting crag, he had a view
Of a huge castle, and full well he knew
That 'twas Sir Leoline's, whose banner bright
Waved insolent in his astonished sight.
And Richard's wandering musings all were chased,
And were at once by boundless hate replaced.
Unknowingly he'd strayed on the domain
Of his born foe, and stood, with raging brain,

The Antiquary's Tale.

Filled with that strongest hate which knows its foe,
But not what quarrel 'tis which makes it so.
His fist he raised, his teeth he tightly ground,
And, angry growling, sudden heard a sound
Of footsteps near; 'twas good! what joy to fight
Some foe, and slay, or put him unto flight.
He turned, and, in the path which here did meet
With his, there stood a beauteous maiden sweet,
Tall, fair, and graceful, noble in her mien,
The loveliest creature he had ever seen.
Oh! rich warm hair, fair face, and sweet kind eyes,
Why should ye fill a youth with such surprise?
When he the bravest, strongest man would fight,
Why should a gentle maid put him to flight?
A modest blush was o'er her face diffused,
She seemed with his embarrassment amused,
Yet, as he looked, he thought, but scarce knew why,
'Mid pride, there was a kindness in her eye.
Clumsy he moved his hat from off his head,
And words apologetic stammerèd.
"Sir, by your dress, you noble seem to be,
And, if you've lost your way, my father, he
Who dwells in yonder castle——" "Lady, stay,
No more dare I to hear, nor more to say,
And yet——" He turned, a sigh of pain arose,
Then warm he spoke, "Why, why should we be foes?
Say, say, oh! say that me thou dost not hate."
"Foes," she half breathless said, "why, what debate,
What hatred may there be between us two?
No hate is mine, what hate should be in you?"

"Madame, Sir Roland, Lord of Tryermaine,
My father is." "Alas! 'tis sad, again
I hear of one whom I dare never name
Unto my father; thee, oh! fate, I blame,
That cruel thing, whatever it may be,
That 'twixt our fathers has thrust enmity."
And now her look was sad, her smile was fled,
She was not angry; nay, she'd more have said,
Have told him danger was around him here,
Have wished him fortune in his knight's career,
Wished that they were not foes, might friendly be;
All this he plainly in her face could see,
Her beauteous face, now moved with feelings kind,
Flown from the heart and governed by the mind.
And, ever going, unprepared to go,
Stood these young folks, each one the other's foe.
Longer he must not stay on foeman's land,
Now they'd for ever part. He held his hand
With a half diffidence, with pleading look,
And hers she held not back, as it he took
A new-found wish in his whole being rose,
Which all his doubtings did for ever close.
He loved, he told her, pleaded then his cause
With fervent eloquence which knew no pause.
She listened, blushed, moved not, nor once did chide;
She could not, for she loved. What shall betide
With such a love, a love that's thus begun?
What might they think? Think? Their two hearts in one
Ne'er doubted for the future, nor could say
How near or distant was that happy day

When trials should be passed, and their love true
No more, in fear, should hide itself from view.

Strange that one thought will often hold a sway
Over two distant minds, far, far away.
Thus, with Sir Roland and Sir Leoline,
One thought would oft around their two minds twine.
'Twas hate, into intensest feeling wrought,
Yet would not wrong the other, e'en in thought.
It was a hate that all on honour stood,
Wished not to be appeased by shedding blood,
Wished not for injury, revenge, or woe,
But only that it could forget its foe.
Had they but known what in their very blood
Had been enacted, strange had been their mood.
Yet each one oft a searching, puzzled look
Cast on his child; could it be, in some nook
Of that young heart, some secret there might be?
And this strange thought oppressed them frequently.

Sir Leoline, that mighty baron rich,
Hath, as you know, a toothless mastiff bitch.
Of this you in the poet's verse have read;
That poet with imagination fed
With strange weird thoughts which oft the mind astound,
Whilst, 'mid them, loveliest images abound,
He tells how, one night in the early year,
When the impassive moon shone cold and clear,
The mastiff, near her kennel, in sound sleep,
Uttered a lowly moan of anger deep,

As Christabel crossed o'er the courtyard wide,
With Geraldine, the beauteous, by her side,
Whom she had met as she, distressed, did roam,
And had, in pity, brought unto her home.
What meant the mastiff's moan? It had been well
If to her room the gentle Christabel
Had never ta'en the wicked Geraldine,
Who against Christabel had ill design,
And, in her plot, now felt herself secure
To harm the maid, so innocent and pure,
Whose sleep was broken by a warning dream,
While Geraldine's sleep free from care did seem.

Next morning Christabel sought Leoline,
And unto him brought the fair Geraldine,
Who told her tale of woe. The baron heard
In silence, then his heart was deeply stirred.
"What! Thou the daughter of my long-lost friend,
Sir Roland? Good. Ah! now our hate will end.
Oh! good and noble Roland, true as steel
Thou ever wast; shall thy dear daughter heal
Our feud? Yea, maiden, thou art good as fair.
Bard Bracy, to Sir Roland quick repair,
Thank him for message from his heart so true,
Say swift I come old friendship to renew."
But Bracy never for one moment took
From off fair Geraldine his searching look,
For he, from any power that there might be
In her beguiling beauty, was quite free;

Nor smile from her e'er won him; nor dark look,
Nor pleading glance, his faithfulness once shook.
And then he told the baron he had dreamed
Last night he in the woods saw, as it seemed,
A fluttering dove, which was his daughter dear,
A foul snake coiled around it, with head near
To the sweet dove's, and thought such dream must tell
Of danger near to Lady Christabel.
Impatient heard the baron, for the sign
Shown by the dream he wrongly did divine.
Then, with authority, bade Bracy heed
His words, and quickly on his message speed.

Bracy went forth; and on his errand sped.
Grimly to him Sir Roland answerèd,
"Ho! Hath Lord Leoline some witch received,
By vile enchantment hath he been deceived?
Bid him not be beguiled by cursèd sleight
Of soul-destroying imp from realm of night.
No daughter have I, no, nor ever had."
Away rode Bracy. Ah! his heart was sad.
His dream, Geraldine's looks, Sir Roland's speech,
Increased his fears, he wished at once to reach
The castle, and to tell his lord how he
In danger was of man's great enemy.
Yet how persuade that baron and his child,
Both by such seeming-goodness so beguiled?
Soon as the hall he gained, his master fell
Into swift speech, "Hear, now, what I've to tell!

Soon as thou startedst forth, that Geraldine
Said, 'Subtly traitorous is that bard of thine,
And high should hang.' It stung me to the heart
To hear thy good faith slighted. Oh! what smart
It gave to me. I told her that my choice
Thou wast for deeds of trust. With sweeter voice,
That seemed to lull, and gentlest mood would bring,
She spoke nor good nor ill, yet e'er did cling
Around thy name, as if thou hurtful were
Unto herself. 'Lady,' said I, 'I swear
E'en by the Holy Cross——' Ere I could end
She, shuddering, turned away. Then did I send
For Fulke the chaplain, whilst, to me, she said
She'd in the chapel pray; but, ah! she fled.
Fulke found her not; we searched; the warder told
She'd through the gateway passed; and Edric, bold,
Fearful of nought, from the moors trembling came,
And said that he had seen the beauteous dame
With five strange knights, on horses swift as wind,
And of such form as ne'er, unto his mind,
He'd ever seen; all went with rapid flight,
And soon were o'er the moors and out of sight.
Oh! Bracy, this is strange. Thou faithful one,
But for thy faith we'd been by spell undone.
But, stranger still, my Christabel has told
Me that she loves the son of Roland bold.
It cannot be; it must not, must not be.
Who knows but some new spell of witchery
May be in this? I troubled am and grieved;
Such thing as this I could not have believed."

So Christabel her Richard now no more
Dare meet. Why came she not? he asked, as sore
Fell this hard blow. He could half guess its cause.
Then to his father, after many a pause,
He told his grief. Lord Roland sternly frowned,
Some better fate he hoped he might have found
Than thus so complicated he should be,
And by his son too, with an enemy.
" 'Tis well ye're parted, foolish youngsters both,
Hard though it is to break from plighted troth,
Yet, with your minds to sense returned, ye'll find
Partners who round you blissful peace will bind."

Lord Galbin was a baron who lived far
From Roland and from Leoline. In war
He ever sought to plunge, whene'er it moved
Him to some conquest, though he fighting loved
For its own sake, so did his children too,
And they were many, but their instinct true
E'er led them where they some reward might gain,
That fighting's pleasure were not pleasure vain.
They'd oft drive off some neighbour's kine or
    sheep,
And many a rich man's goods they'd seize and keep.
If he complained, they'd offer then to fight
With him for what was his, as if their right
He had transgressed, as if his property
Were prize for any one who'd for it try.
And, in the hurly-burly of their life,
Two of his sons had fallen in the strife,

But four were left, who his lieutenants were,
Well pleased in dangers of his wars to share.
His seven daughters for dominion sighed,
And, seeking husbands rich, went far and wide.
And four had gained, and ruled them, saving one
Who'd o'er her sullen lord no victory won,
Then warned (as she said, for her sex's sake)
All girls that marriage was a great mistake.
Noisy, thrusting, grasping, fond of threat
Were father, mother, sons, and daughters ; set
On one design, that they'd make all things theirs
By fight, or taking foe at unawares.

Lord Galbin sits in hall, the platters smoke,
The flagons pass around, the cheerful joke
And jovial laugh are heard, and all are gay ;
For one, at least, it is a happy day ;
It is for Walter, Galbin's youngest son,
Who sits beside the maiden he has won,
Who soon will be his bride, fair Geraldine,
Soon to be wedded to the Galbin line.
Demure she sat, as Lady Galbin's eye
Was fixed on her, to see if she could spy
Aught was ungentle in her looks or voice,
Or weak, unworthy of a Galbin's choice ;
Scarce satisfied with all Geraldine's ways,
Though there was nothing which she could not
    praise.
At last, aloud, " What may thy proud sire say
Unto this match ? " " My sire, Lord Roland ? Nay.

And yet he is my sire. Then, why in hate
And rage should he thus thrust me from his gate?
O'ercome by spell which makes him think that I,
His daughter, am some witch. Ah! where to fly
I knew not, but a friend came to my aid,
So kind, so good, and long with her I've stayed."
Fast flowed her silent tears, then ceasing, she,
Resigned, seemed to forgive; for sympathy
She glanced around, and, in one moment, took
Their faces and their thoughts in that meek look.
"My fame, aspersed, would soon all guileless stand
If fairly tried. Although Lord Roland's land
Is wide and fertile, his retainers few
Could hardly hold the field, but if he knew
How he has wronged me, sure his knighthood high
Would swift to any reparation fly."

Lord Galbin looked, and looked, Lord Galbin heard.
His soul down to its lowest depth was stirred.
Here was a chance for profitable fight,
For gaining fame in quarrel which seemed right,
P'rhaps show the king that he'd a good cause ta'en,
And thus Lord Roland's lands and title gain.
His sons, with greatest joy, then heard him tell
He'd march against Lord Roland; ah! 'twas well;
To them would surely fall a goodly spoil,
And they'd have prizes after martial toil.

Now the retainers mustered for the fray.
Men, by the late war ruined, joined, for pay,

Lord Galbin's mighty army; every knight
That held a fee of him, all he could cite
To come, came with his vassals in the field,
Where many a visored helmet, kite-shaped shield
Showed cognisance of gentleman or knight,
And gonfanons, and blazoned banners bright,
Borne by the ring-mailed warriors, waved on high
O'er spearmen, billmen, archers, cavalry.
Slow moved the mass of troops, the hills around
Re-echo with the trumpet's stirring sound,
And deep drums, urging on to warlike deed.
The soldiers' spirits rise as they proceed.
Young knights, with loved one's sleeve in helmet bright,
With joy survey their troops, and long for fight;
While older knights, who've many a battle seen,
Though cheerful, yet ride on with sober mien,
Glad that good spirit moves the armèd band,
But wish to hold that spirit well in hand
Lest it o'erflow, and, weakening discipline,
Instead of beating foes, cause foes to win.

Lord Roland's vassals all were brave, and true
Unto their cause, but were in number few
Compared with those who under Galbin fought,
So aid from Oterville Lord Roland sought.
Lord Oterville had all the warrior's fire,
But was much influenced by his giddy squire,
Young Paradis de Foule, a butterfly,
A fop who, with small talk of matters high,

Thought that of everything much more he knew
Than practised men who everything could do.
So, when Lord Oterville had promised aid,
His preparations were so long delayed,
That Roland was compelled to go to war
Alone, lest Galbin should advance too far.
He anxiously and seriously thought
Of battle 'gainst superior forces fought,
Yet thus must be fought, for his land, his life,
Hung in those balances whose beam was strife.
And heavy was the heart of his young son,
Who'd long been parted from his dear loved one.
Life to him all was dark, not faintest ray,
Amidst its gloom, gave hope of brighter day;
And, when most wishing that he might remove
The heavy clouds that hung around his love,
Then gentle thoughts must fly, and stern ones reign
O'er dreary life, and add unto its pain.

Sir Roland took the field, and met the foe.
The armies faced each other; grand the show
Of ranks of massèd men with bows and spears;
And from each army rise defiant cheers.
"My son," said Roland, "ere begins the fight,
This I would say; to-day full many a knight
Will meet his death. Oh! Richard, this may be
The last time we'll, on earth, each other see.
We may all scathless fight, or both, or one
  Be slain. Should I now fall, 'twill be, my son,

For thee to lead; none better could I choose,
In thy true hands bright honour nought will lose.
Yet"—here he paused; "thoughts of old days entwine
Themselves with present thoughts. On Leoline
I much have mused, as if, within my mind,
There came, unsought, memory of nature kind
And friendship warm, were his. If now, to me,
Death should be near, and it, perhaps, may be,
I'd beg forgiveness of Sir Leoline,
Sure he'd not question if the fault were mine,
His noble heart would instantly respond
To the first uttered word of friendship fond.
Whate'er our quarrel, may it buried be,
Too long, too great, has been my enmity;
It now is dead. And may his daughter, she
Whom thou dost love, share love's pure bliss with thee.
May, too, the clouds which darken now your fate
Be soon dispersed, and may the fathers' hate
Be, by the children, turned to love again,
And, through long happy life e'er, constant, reign."

Then rode he through the ranks, gave each his post,
Spoke words encouraging throughout the host.
The archers mustered and began the fight,
And arrows would on shields and helmets light,
Then, coming nearer, shafts would pierce the mail,
And men began to fall, and rage assail
Those who still lived, seeing friends who'd yielded breath,
With once bright face now colourless in death.

Cruel destruction governed every mind,
And every weapon would a victim find,
And fierce the press, and strangest noise arose
Of shouts, and groans, and cries, and clank of blows
Mixed in one din confused, where limbs and lives
Were cheaply held, where Death or Injury drives
Good bargains with fell Discord, till they see
Fatigue will, for awhile, stop butchery.
Here many a youthful knight or squire first won
His fame, while many a veteran was undone;
And many a youth of promise came to grief
Who would not to old counsel give belief.
Lord Galbin slowly, with his numbers great,
Advantage gained; Lord Roland hoped, though late,
All might be yet retrieved; his heaviest horse
He ranged and, leading, charged with all his force;
A fearful shock! Unhorsed was many a wight,
But, when he could, still kept, on foot, the fight.
Then came another troop, by Galbin sent,
And they were fresh, the others' strength half spent.
Yet still with courage fought Lord Roland's men,
And he, too, battled marvellously, but, when
He'd many slain, a spearman thrust him through.
Against great odds, what could small numbers do?
And, when he fell, his men soon lost all heart,
While their swift-charging enemies would part
Their ranks, and turn their flight quick into rout.
And news of Roland's death soon flew about
And broke his men up, for, while some would fly
On hearing it, some fought more desperately;

But all their desperation was in vain,
It brought exhaustion and, to foes, was gain.
While Richard, reckless, desperate, meant to close
His life, wild fighting 'mid surrounding foes,
But an old squire, 'mongst those who near were found,
His bridle seized, and turned his charger round.

Ill-ended fight that was so well begun.
Lord Galbin's numerous troops the field had won,
And rested on it, filled with triumph high,
Though at great cost they'd bought their victory.
Fell one of Galbin's sons, 'twas Walter, keen
In fight, the news was brought to Geraldine,
And, as she heard, she shed her easy tears,
O'erborne by sorrow and by bitter fears.
"All joy of life now lost," she sighed, "how sweet
Were death, 'twould lay me at my loved one's feet."
Demurely she looked round for sympathy,
And, as each face passed 'neath her scrutiny,
On bold Sir Robert lingeringly cast
Her eye, and knew that now she held him fast
Within her toils, and that she still might play
Her baneful game on mischief's widening way.

Not far off from the battle-field there stood
A little manor-house, 'twas near a wood.
Brave Leoline, who had a visit paid
To this lone house, now with its owner stayed,
As something like a score of Galbin's men,
Loose hangers-on, who'd come out of some den

Of robbers, who disorder loved, and spoil,
Nor cared for discipline or steady toil,
Came toward the manor-house in hope of prey,
To steal or wreck whatever came their way.
The host urged flight; Sir Leoline roared, "No!
I never turned my back to any foe.
Bolt thou the door, and——" More he would have said,
But coward host and timid servants fled.
He closed the bolts. "My Christabel, fear nought.
In many a fiercer fight than this I've fought
With manly foes, and ne'er have run away,
And these vile thieves shall give me no dismay.
Weep not, my girl, thy father's arm is stout,
True and brave foes it hath put to the rout
Full oft." With jarring noise the door was split,
The foe with axe had roughly broken it.
It soon was hewed away; the first man in,
Was slain at once, cut through from crown to chin.
The second fell, when one, more in the rear,
Through Leoline's leg thrust his hateful spear.
Though great his pain, he still dealt sturdy blows,
And fighting, wounded, often felled his foes,
Till, weak with loss of blood, he down did fall,
And conquerors' yell resounded through the hall.

One had seized Christabel, and held her fast
Throughout the fray, and now, the combat past,
With terror filled, with father slaughtered, she
Struggled, from him who held her, to be free,

In vain, and swift from scene of the affray,
In furious mood he hurried her away.
Vain were her shrieks, all vainly she implored,
When, on a sudden, she espied his sword,
As he, suspectless, thought she was his prey,
She seized the hilt, and snatched his sword away.
He loosed his hold, and, as his hand he put
To seize her wrist, she, with a reckless cut,
Took from his hand three fingers, and then fled,
Whilst the maimed wretch howled loudly as he bled.
Swiftly she ran, and far, nor knew her way,
Though tirèd, panting, yet dared never stay,
Till of a market-woman, met by chance,
She askèd aid. The dame a fearful glance
Cast on her—was she witch, or sprite abhorred,
This breathless beauty carrying bloody sword?
At last, assured, she gave to Christabel
A seat behind her, then rode o'er the fell,
Forced from the road, which Galbin's men had ta'en,
And, turning from their course, reached Tryermaine.

And here, next morn, Richard met Christabel.
They could but sad news to each other tell.
Both orphaned in one day, with nought to assuage
Defeated Richard, full of gloomy rage.
Long parted love, now met, should scarce be coy,
But should, methinks, o'erflow with tender joy.
Love now but spoke of grief, of danger too,
With a victorious foe almost in view,

With doubts if Richard still could keep the field,
Or, closed in castle walls, at length must yield.
With fear his friend might come too late in day,
Lord Oterville, slow lagging on the way.
Sudden the thought occurred to Christabel,
She'd haste unto her castle, and would tell
Her men to march, that Richard might oppose,
With equal numbers, his so numerous foes.
" I'll send all, saving those, I'll take a few
To seek my murdered father———" feeble grew
Her voice, tears drowned it, she no more could say,
But turned and, sudden, hurried away.

With escort small, she to the castle sped.
Near it she saw, with wonder, fear, and dread,
A litter borne by men, some four or five,
And on it lay—her father? Yes, alive!
Was this some miracle? At once she sped
To him, who seemed as if raised from the dead.
But he was feeble with the loss of blood,
And in despondent, miserable mood.
" Father, forgive me, that I ran away,
Thou seemedst dead as there I saw thee lay,
And brutish hands were laid on me, in fright,
To save my honour 'twas I took to flight."
Bright beamed the baron's eye. " Thou'rt safe, my
    dear.
My wound pains much; but far worse was my fear;
For fear I've had, as of thy fate I've thought.
But thou art safe, thank God, for He has brought

Thee out of danger. Now, anxiety
Hath left me, wounds will never trouble me.
Whose be these gallant lads who've hither sped?"
" They're Lord de Vaux's." " Eh! What?" he, snarling,
   said.
And then she told him of Lord Roland's death,
And how he'd blessed his friend with his last breath,
And how she'd fled and come to Tryermaine,
And—swift the baron, with a cry of pain
And rage, turned on her; words availed her not,
They but inflamed the baron's rage so hot.
He feebly blustered, " In the very nick
Of evil time there ever comes some trick.
No doubt that cursèd woman Geraldine
Was sent by Roland on some vile design,
And caused confusion that will never end.
And—he is dead. Well, well, he was my friend.
But thou, beholden to his caitiff son;
Against my best designs full tilt to run!"
His rage, his anguish, failing strength, and pain
O'erbore the warrior, and his pride, in vain,
'Gainst nature struggled; faintness took away
Power, and he long in dangerous illness lay.

There comes a time when all that we have done
Has been in vain, we have no victory won,
But aye have lost, and strong victorious foes,
Certain of final conquest, round us close;
Some thought arises, it is scarce a hope,
That we shall with our difficulties cope,

And with success ; it is not confidence
Which now we have ; it is some passive sense
Which makes us to all loss resigned, that we
To seize on every 'vantage now are free.
Now Richard felt that all his hope was gone,
But one more fight and he must be undone.
His father, loved one, gone, his warfare vain,
Soon would his lands, e'en life, from him be ta'en.
Yet when he saw his men's cool courage true,
All free from fear of what the foe might do ;
And heard that plunder had debased his foe,
(Discordant force, true men and rascals low,)
He thought that if—and then came hope again,
But hope with "if"; it might be hope in vain.
His men he posted on a rising ground.
Best spirit was in all his army found.
But, as the foe drew near, their numbers great
Appalled him, though he steadily did wait
Their onset, and repulsed it, waited then
Their next attack ; 'twas made with fewer men ;
And soon he learned the cause ; he heard the din
Of battle on his left. He now would win,
Since Oterville had come unto his aid,
At length he'd brought the help so long delayed.
Then flashed his mind in flame ; that hope, had lain
Imprisoned, burst its bonds, and flight had ta'en
Swift through his men, they charged with hearty will,
And broke their foes, and drove them down the hill.
There others hemmed them in, and there much rage
Was spent, as foes so savage did engage ;

Here ranks were mixed, mingled were foe and
    friend,
And many a warrior's life came to an end,
And there lay many slain, there weapons, blood,
And limbs cut off in fray around were strewed.
But rage at last must tire, when courage stout,
By strong foes undismayed, will still hold out,
So Galbin's men at length were forced to yield,
And, by their foes, were driven from off the field.

Lord Oterville, though late, had not held back.
He'd drawn off many from the fierce attack
Was made on Richard. But the foeman quick
Upon him sprang, before his mass so thick
Of troops he could arrange, and drove them in,
And broke their ranks, and fast began to win.
Who had seen him would strange emotions trace
In every feature of his heavy face.
Gazing upon his troopers' broken rows,
His fat moustache, his thick-set Roman nose,
His baggy cheeks, and proud lack-lustre eyes,
Seemed all aghast, filled with one huge surprise.
His men driven back ! He scarcely could believe
What he did see ; yet there, nought could deceive
Where all was clear ; his men were full in flight.
All had been lost, had not one brave old knight
Held well his post, and bade his men stand fast,
Hurried to Oterville, and begged him cast
His lighter troops upon the foeman's wing ;
Thus from confusion he did order bring,

And, asking leave, he really did command,
Packed broken ranks, and made a goodly stand.
Then charged the heavy horse in time of need,
And Oterville, none braver mounted steed,
Led them himself, his mighty form was seen
Dealing out death with heavy faulchion keen.
And, in the thick of fight, came Richard's men
Victorious, and fell on Galbin's; then
O'erpowered they fell back, and, ere long, their might
Was broken, humbled, and soon lost in flight.

Great was the rout, great were the numbers slain,
And many a gallant knight was prisoner ta'en,
Bringing rich ransom to the victor lords,
While plunder the brave soldiers' toil rewards.
Now blood was up, how many did advise
To march on Galbin's lands, that glorious prize.
But Richard's vassals, who had fought for life,
Wished now to plunge no deeper into strife;
Their foe laid low, they wanted now to address
Themselves unto their hindered business.
Lord Oterville, though brave, was fond of ease,
And the late fight had been enough to please
His present humour. And, for Richard, well,
What made him pause? What was it? Need I tell?

Now victory beyond all doubt; the foe
In full retreat, broken, with pride laid low,
Agreed to peace, and hostages did give
That peace they'd keep as long as each should live.

Oh! such a peace, so ratified and sealed,
All future cause of discord should have healed.
But whether these good terms were kept as they
Were made, is much more than I dare to say.

Long lay Sir Leoline, faint, sick, and weak,
But had recovered, could he only speak
Calmly of what had happened since began
My tale, he cou'd not, it did him unman.
His rage, his pride, his valour, all assailed
His sturdy spirit, which to foe ne'er quailed,
But drooped 'neath their assaults; he only knew
How they told on him as he weaker grew.
Weak, ill! or he'd have challenged young de Vaux.
A daughter's love won by a hated foe!
And he quite helpless, she his constant nurse.
Her duty, her affection, seemed like curse
Upon his plans; her heart, he well did know,
Strayed over bordering land to young de Vaux.
He saw her face, oh! "fair, not pale," as said
The poet, with its beauty ravishèd.
But now 'twas pale, 'twas faint; he heard her sighs,
He watched her when she'd hardly meet his eyes,
And knew she was absorbed in thoughts of one,
Richard, his foe! Then would the fever run
Fierce through his veins and weakness would succeed,
While Christabel, e'er ready at his need,
Soothed him, and watched, and gave the kindly word
So good in season, while her poor heart, stirred

With love, with care, with grief, seemed dark, seemed dead,
No light could e'er again be o'er it shed.
Full well that weak, that helpless father knew
How dutiful she was, but heart's love grew
On soil was nourished by an enemy,
This was his bitterest cause of misery.
He had commanded her to throw away
All thought of love for Richard. "Father, stay,"
She said, "until you're well, ere this you ask."
"Eh! What?" the baron growled, "a pretty task
You promise, girl, that you'll you're father give;
You shall not have him, no, sure as I live;
And I will live, ha! and grow strong again,
And then we'll fight till one of us be slain."
"But, father, think, not dangerous your wound;
A little rest will make you hale and sound.
My love for you incessant urges on
All power, all skill I have; there shall be done
The best that I can do to make you well.
Such is your daughter's love. You, sure, can tell
I love you as a daughter; then, as wife,
As truly I should love, and, as my life
Is bound to father and to lover both,
I will not break away from plighted troth.
I dare not leave him who so loveth me,
E'en as, at his desire, I'd not leave thee.
Oh! such a thought one moment in his brain
He'd ne'er allow. Dear father, not again
Ask this of me. I promise you, howe'er
Long time your illness last, that I will ne'er

To Richard speak, nor any token send
To him against your wish. You I'll still tend
With heart, with hand, trusting to ease your pain.
Trouble not, father, you shall ne'er complain
Of act of mine. I must, I will, be true
To Richard ; but, dear father, I'll ne'er do
Aught 'gainst your wish. Have then no doubt of me,
And you'll from illness be the sooner free."

Silenced, but unconvinced, the baron turned
Uneasy in his bed, while hotly burned
His oft ignited brain. "A pretty task,"
He murmured o'er and o'er, and when would ask
His daughter, priest, or leech, what he might mean,
He'd grimly smile, and say, " When comes between
Two young hearts but a little spark of love—
Well, well, we'll see ; this will a business prove.
She will not cross my will ; no, only waits
Until I'm well, and then—well, p'rhaps the fates
May kinder be to them than now they think.
I daily weaker grow ; I'm on the brink,
I feel it, of that weakness which brings down
The strongest to the weakest level ; flown
Soon will my spirit be, unless between
Me and pale death some marvel intervene.
I bar their way ; but when upon my bier
I shall be laid, their road will then be clear,
And then, be sure, their marriage will be near."

Bad was the fever, tortured was his mind,
And the fierce warrior, all unresigned

To lingering illness, daily weaker grew,
While Christabel, in her devotion true
To all his needs, with anxious care and pain
O'ertasked, 'mid work's, love's, duty's trying strain,
Provoked the leech's thought. "She is not well,"
He said; "such care doth much on young hearts tell.
Parted from lover, while her father's strength
Falls, daily, lower; such deep grief at length
Will be too much; I'll move him, or 'twill kill
Father and daughter both. How bend his will?"

He had no need. Next day Sir Leoline
Beckoned his daughter. Low she did incline
Her head to catch his whisper, hardly more
Could he now utter. "Christabel, before
I leave this world, I fain would make all well.
He may be thine. Fetch Bracy, bid him tell
Young Lord de Vaux hither to come with speed.
Oh! were I well enough to mount a steed,
I'd challenge him; but, ah! it may not be.
I cannot part two hearts. But I would see
That foe, that son of foe, and I will speak
My heart out to him; ere I be too weak
I'll rouse my strength. I die, it must be so,
But it shall be with face against my foe."

Ah! Who can say what thoughts poor Christabel
Had at these words? She felt that she could tell
Her father she'd from young de Vaux be free,
If but her sire in health again might be.

Yet, not to vex him, not opposed his will.
She vainly, vainly bade her heart be still,
And sent for Bracy, and the message gave.
Away rode Bracy, ah! his thoughts were grave.
Though fast he sped, yet hoped he for no good
From this occurrence; nought of blessing could
From disobedience come, so on he rode,
Swiftly, with beating heart which did forbode
Some greater ill beneath the present pain,
So galloped fast to ease his troubled brain.
And, reaching Tryermaine, learned that its lord
Was in the church at Mass, nor would accord
Audience to any till the Mass was said,
Nor wished it Bracy, although thus delayed
His message was, but to the church he went,
And joined in worship of the Sacrament.

The beauteous Geraldine had tired of sin,
Had found it false, and now wished to begin
To try if she could lead a better life;
She longed for peace, she weary was of strife.
Repentance she had o'er and o'er delayed,
And, wandering aimlessly, had hither strayed.
She followed Bracy; yet she knew not why;
But he not once looked round, so that his eye
Never met hers; that was, for her, as well;
For, had he seen her, who is there can tell
What indignation fierce he had exprest
To her, who'd been his master's viper-guest?

She saw him enter church, she followed
Into the churchyard, and, when there, strange dread
Possessed her, on she could not go, nor back
Could turn ; her mind now seemed upon the rack.
In anguish deep, she by the church-wall stood,
Thinking of days of innocence, how good
She might have been, but now, so black and foul
With filth of sin that darkly stained her soul.
At times she heard the words the priest pronounced,
At times responses ; or a pause announced
Some part well known in days long left behind,
Now brought no peace, but seemed to craze her mind.
The tears rolled down her cheeks, the frowns of pain
Misshaped her features ; o'er and o'er again
She sank upon her knees, again uprose,
She thought some foe unseen dealt staggering blows.
But when she heard the priest's voice, solemn, clear,
Say, " Hoc est corpus Meum," then, what fear
Possessed her wholly ; sinking on the ground,
She, in the hollows 'tween green graves around,
Wriggled, like some foul snake, in dread and pain,
Then swooned, and lay on earth as one was slain.

The Mass at end, forth through the church-porch
    stray
The folk. The first saw where Geraldine lay
All torpid in the grass, and to her aid,
With others, went, and all looked on dismayed
At sight so strange, and wondered how came there
Such beauteous dame clad in rich garments rare.

Last came the priest, passed through the opening press;
And Geraldine, now strengthened, did address.
"Who art thou, daughter, and what grief hast thou?"
But Bracy, all impatient, shouted, "How
Darest thou appear, thou witch?" At this dread word
Wild terror every man and woman stirred;
They started from her side, while she sank low
Down on her knees, o'ercome by deepest woe.
"Oh! father, is there hope?" she meekly said.
"Yea, daughter," said the priest, "whate'er hath led
Thy steps this way, or whatsoe'er thy life
Hath been, yet know the way from sinful strife
To heavenly peace is ever offered;
For, though our sins as scarlet have been red,
They shall be white as snow, if we but take
That road which our dear Lord for us did make.
He ever urges sinners to repent
And be in one with Him; His good word sent
To us doth ever call us to His side,
For, whatsoe'er our sins, how deep, how wide,
What are they to His love? Then with faith move
Thy heart, amend thy life, and win that love."

Then Geraldine rose slowly to her feet,
And, with a downcast look, in accents sweet,
She asked, "Oh! father, can I, sure, be saved?"
"Thou askest," said the priest, "what some have braved
To offer, but the minister am I
To do God's will, and dare for nothing try

Save what He granted to me, when the vow
Of priest I took. But, daughter, listen, how
Thou mayest be His ; submit thee to His will,
Who dwells among His people alway till
The world doth end, thou wilt with Him abide,
And He with thee, and, ever at His side,
What canst thou have of doubt, what fear, when He
Is ever with thee, dearest Friend to be ?
Oh! child of clay, unto His will submit,
He doth invite thee, were there ever writ
Such words of love as His ? Cast off thy sin,
And by the narrow pathway enter in."

With downcast look poor Geraldine had heard,
While many a sigh had oft her bosom stirred.
Now meekly, gently, penitent, she raised
Her eyes, and full upon the kind priest gazed.
Yet spoke she not, while those around her there
For the poor sinner breathed a silent prayer.
Steady the priest looked in her face, to win
Her thought and free her from her deadly sin.
Hard was his look, her sin he sought to tear
Out by its root, yet for that creature fair
Felt deepest pity, striving he might bring
Her to the Lord of love, great mercy's King.
Keen was the look of each, and, when she saw
No admiration she from him could draw,
She, sudden, threw her arms up in the air,
Then jerked them down, and round did fiercely stare,

And loud and harshly laughed, then snatched her dress,
And fled with swiftest speed, while the whole press
Were numbed with terror, some did faint, some screamed;
'Twas as if grisly horror they had dreamed
Were realized. But fearless John o' Hove
Drew sword and chased her, while none dared to move
From the churchyard till he came back, his sword
With unstained blade. At first he scarce one word
Could speak, but, calmer grown, at length he said,
"I followed her full fast, she quickly fled,
And, though I ever gained, she kept ahead.
Her even strength seemed as 'twould ne'er be spent,
Out on the heathy moor at length she went;
There, where the Druid stones in circle stand,
She flew into their midst, I reached my hand,
I almost touched her, as around one stone
She ran; in instant I was all alone,
Nor anywhere around me could I see
That cursèd witch." Then one cried out with glee,
"Oh! Jack, we know you, you can always tell
Such tales as that." "Hush," said the priest, "'tis well
That she is gone." Then all went to their home,
And never near the Druid stones would roam.
Nor ever more did beauteous Geraldine
Visit that spot; but some of those who'd seen
(So they would tell) at night the demon hounds
And horses, headless, fly o'er the hunting grounds
On the wild moors, as if in chase of sport,
Had heard, 'mid hunters' cry, 'mid horses' snort,

That harsh, rough laugh, by all rememberèd,
Which pierced their ears, as when Geraldine fled.

Lord Richard and Bard Bracy rode away.
Grave were their thoughts, they scarce one word could
    say.
What happiness was given to Richard now,
Yet mingled with such grief; in death lay low
His much-loved father; and Sir Leoline,
His friend at last, toward death did now decline.
They reached the castle-gate, the servants told
Their lord was calm; on Bracy's heart how cold
This news fell; now the end seemed drawing near,
The trusty bard felt faint with anxious fear,
So quickly made his way unto his lord,
And told him Richard waited on his word.
" Bring him," the baron said, with little grace,
A hard stern look was on his martial face,
And in his heart hot fierce emotions burned,
As Richard came, his back was toward him turned.
And Christabel (one moment barely) took
Her eye from his set face to meet the look
Of love her Richard gave; for pain upon
Their two hearts had the victory almost won
O'er love; at once again upon her sire
She looked and saw th' unyielding rage and ire
She'd seen when, facing many a burly foe,
He'd stood his ground and given back blow for blow.
Sharply her fingers laced, her two arms tight
Pressed 'gainst her side, while set her lips so white,

As slow the baron turned upon his side,
With look in which there seemed intensified
His heart, his soul, when he on Richard cast
His piercing, unquailed eye—then, all aghast,
He stared, dismayed, the fiery warrior fled.
He faintly gasped, "Thou here? But no; the dead
Come not again—and yet—how may this be?"
He reached his hand, and Richard, on his knee,
With hand in his, heard his now gentle voice,
"Youth, thou art like thy father, I rejoice
That ere I die, I see thee; all the grace
Of the De Vaux's is thine; thy father's face
Thou hast, I thought thou wast himself; the look
He wore when first on battlefield we took
Our place, is thine; his glance on me was kind,
The best of feelings filled his noble mind,
He wished me victory, honour, and success,
And much rejoiced when fame my deeds did bless.
Those moments all came back as I saw thee;
My rage is ended; love alone shall be
Chain of my heart and thine, thy father's too,
For, though between us both a difference grew,
I loved him ever, and am sure his love,
As mine, though hurt, could never feeble prove.
But I grow weak, and we may talk too long.
Come hither, Christabel; and now the wrong
Which I have done, I'll mend. My daughter dear
Here take to be thy bride. And may love cheer
Your path with richest blessings. Can love die?
No; nought can kill it; oft we view awry

Its perfect form, and think 'tis full of fault,
As we against its perfectness revolt.
And may the fathers' love, though broken long,
By children re-united, grow more strong.
But I must rest, my strength is now outrun;
Retire, I fain would sleep, my work is done."

Sadly the lovers left the baron's room.
This trying day had ta'en away the bloom
Of love for them; full of uneasiness,
It seemed as if they'd brought on this distress
Which had so weakened Leoline; while he
Slept well, now freed from all anxiety.
"Thus he will pass away," the leech would tell
At each inquiry made by Christabel.
Slowly the long hours passed. The lovers two
Half happy, were full sad; their love so true,
And tried, victorious, mingled with such pain,
Caused by their love, from them all joy had ta'en.
Love seemèd like some beauteous flower, where
The finest leaves are torn; 'tis spoilt; howe'er
'Tis still a beauteous flower which we prize,
It charms, yet grieves, yet charms our saddened eyes.
For hours and hours he slept, a peaceful sleep,
Evenly breathing in his slumber deep.
At last he turned and tossed, as the leech stood
Near him, then woke, and called aloud for food.
The leech rejoiced, the crisis now was past,
And full recovery would come at last.

Now war, strife, illness, o'er, there came a day
When, in the valley, on the hills away,

The glorious sunlight brightened every scene,
Illumed the blue sky, richer made the green
Of fields, and trees ; and rocks, and leaping streams,
Sparkled in beauty 'neath the sun's bright beams ;
The church's mossy grey walls warmly shone,
And gorgeous-tinted hues were on the stone
Of its worn floor, where'er the sun's warm light
Had thrown rich colour down from windows bright.
And many a noble, many a knight were there,
And there, too, many a beauteous lady fair,
And bridegroom Richard and bride Christabel,
So sweet, so fair. Ah ! who is there could tell,
Had seen her pain, her sorrow, if that he
In that fair face again might joyance see ?
Behold it now, beneath the bridal veil
Blushing, with winning smile that tells the tale
Of dear-bought happiness, of victory
Which faithful love had gained o'er enmity.
Proud happy Richard, leading forth his bride,
Beauteous 'mid beauty, through the pathway wide,
Where her white shining robe and snowy veil
Shone 'mid the beauteous bridesmaids' dresses pale ;
And brave old Leoline, and every guest,
Noble in bearing, sumptuously drest,
Appeared so splendid that there rose in air,
From the great crowd that had assembled there,
A mighty cheer of pleasure at the sight,
Mixed with the deeper joy, that now the right
Had risen o'er wrong which caused it such distress,
And tried true love had now gained happiness.

Prologue to the Spinster's Tale.

As soon as Mr. Antiquary made
An end of his narration, we all paid
Thanks due to him, and said that he
   had told
A goodly tale of mighty days of old,
And shown that love, and pride, and right, and wrong
Were, in the old times, every way as strong
As they are now.   Ah! weak humanity!
That from emotions never can be free,
And, if it could, there would be, there's no doubt,
Nought left for any bard to write about.
And some praised this, some that, as every mind
A character like to itself would find,
But all praised Leoline's so trying part,
His stubborn nature, and his loving heart.

Then spake the Wife of Bath.   "That was," said she,
" A good stout man ; if I again were free,
Why, such an one, in truth, my sixth should be.
What say you, Spinster, what of such a man
Might any woman think?"   "Indeed, I can,"
Replied the Spinster, "never set my mind
Upon such thoughts as yours."   " Ha! could you find,"
Laughed then the Wife, " a partner to your taste,
You'd wed at once, no moments you would waste."

"Well," said the Spinster, "yes, as you just said,
One to my taste; but, oh! to go, and wed
Over and o'er again, as you have done,
Does seem so strange. No sooner fled is one,
Than you another husband seek and gain.
It seems to me, if I might put it plain,
As if the love that lasts, for which all seek,
That can stand trial, that gentle is and meek,
Were scorned by you, and that your only pride
Were the mere boast — a spouse e'er at your side."

"Well now, I'm sure," the Wife of Bath did say,
"This is the way with such as you; my fay,
You ladies, well, I won't be rude, but you
Who don't wed when exactly young, you rue
The fact that you're not married; yes, you know
You do, that's why you carp and cavil so,
And superciliously will talk of men,
Boast of your freedom, blame their tempers, when
You know, if one would only come and ask,
You'd jump with joy to enter on the task
Of marriage; why, of course you would, no doubt,
For that is what all women think about;
You know it is, and those who, in youth's tide,
When glances bring young fellows to their side,
Think winning easy, and must pick and choose,
Find, when too late, how much their time they lose,
And, pick-and-choosing days gone by, they set
Themselves some flouted one to try to get."

"Oh! my; now, did you ever?" said the maid,
"Oh! Wife of Bath, I sadly am afraid
You think all women are alike; not so
It is; for those, like you, whose pride must show
They never will without a husband be,
Must gain, for warmth e'er draws towards warmth, we see.
But would they gain a love that cannot doubt,
That cannot change, and cannot turn about,
But, to one object true, and such would find,
They then seem to be weighing in their mind
(Picking and choosing, as you said just now).
But 'tis not so, indeed 'tis not; for how
Can that be picking, choosing, when we see
All nice, but none that with the heart agree?
While some will wed for wealth, and some for pride,
And some, to get a home, will be a bride,
Some few, with true love gained, will be elate,
But, ah! with such, how oft hard is their fate.
In war the soldier may bid life farewell,
While failure may the trader's hopes dispel,
And, where all seemeth fair, the crafty friend
May cause disruption love can ne'er amend.
E'en peaceful clergy, I have known such case,
On foreign mission sent, may end life's race
When in some trying climate. But, no more
Will I now speak of men. Nought can restore
To a true woman her love once at end,
Through death, misunderstanding, or false friend;
Still, while the hope did last, she e'er would cling
To that which, in the end, much grief did bring,

Yet a blest memory, from which she ne'er
Would part, dead joy amid a living care.
Then has her time gone by, and none arise
To be to her, well, not love's perfect prize,
But one with whom, in kindly sympathy,
The road of life would so much smoother be.
Oh! I have seen brave girls, in families large,
At mother's death have ta'en on them the charge
Of younger sisters, brothers, and the care,
The sense of duty, have from them the air
Of winning ways removed, and far away
Men held from girls so practical; ah! they
Know not what treasure of affection lies
Oft hid 'neath duty's shell; a glorious prize.
And youthful aunts to selves have oft done hurt
When orphaned nephews they would not desert,
Whose parents died and nought have left behind,
And duty made the aunts to orphans kind,
But spoiled their younger life, and left their age
A butt at which poor wits would oft engage.
The peevish and the flirt will drive away
Good men and true, by lightly thinking they
May do whate'er they please, then vainly sigh
When o'ertasked patience makes tired lovers fly.
A friend I had who more than once told me
Her father had enabled her to be
Free from a wife's hard lot, by leaving her
Enough for life; so she was (she'd aver)
Not forced to wed to get a home, and then
She'd no need to submit to nasty men,

Prologue to the Spinster's Tale.

For such she always called them. 'Look,' she'd cry,
'At my poor sisters, scarce one day goes by
But they annoyance from their husbands have;
Look at men's tempers, oh! to be a slave
To tempers only, but in wedlock see
Still greater nuisances from which I'm free.'
Thus, Wife, I trust that I have shown to you
All women do not take the self-same view
Of marriage as yourself." "Tut!" said the Wife.
" They do, but they don't get the chance in life
Which I have had, and used. Ha! ha! Well, well,
Let those who like to think they bear the bell
Of love, if single, widow, think so, I
Like a fresh living spouse." "Oh! Wife, I cry
You mercy, for you're going on too far,"
Exclaimed the Host, " nay, no more wordy war."
And some ado he had to still the Wife,
Whose tongue, now loosed, hankered for tongue-armed
    strife.
Then, turning to the Spinster with a smile
And bow, as if his heart she did beguile,
For she had beauteous been, we all could see,
And took his greeting with an air so free,
It showed she'd been, of old, used to command,
As beauty does, when men are at her hand.
" Lady," said he, " now might I beg of you
Some tale to tell?" " Sir Host, I'll gladly do
The best I can." " Now, thank you, that I hold
Full kind," said Host; and then her tale she told.

The Spinster's Tale.

IN quiet country, far from bustling towns,
There is a little village near the downs,
Where red-tiled roofs all dark with age are seen,
A softened red amid the trees' fair green,
Where all the verdure to the eye is sweet,
Where spring and summer ever seem too fleet;
For one could wish the charm they give the scene
Might always stay; but deeper grows the green,
And the corn ripens, and the autumn hues,
Succeeding gorgeous, tell we soon shall lose
Warmth, brightness, beauty, and we now are near
Cold winter, and the end of one more year.

In spring-time late, when budding leaves are seen,
Showing youth's ardour in their sparkling green
On branches black, relics of winter drear,
'Mid daily growing leaves to disappear,

And wakening nature that around we see
Is bright, half-formed, and full of energy ;
No depth of hue, no wealth of form are there,
But all is growing, moving, strengthening, e'er
Striving to brighten what was dull before,
And upon bareness shed a plenteous store.
Pale flowers in woods, young buds on branches high,
Bright orchard blossoms, and the light blue sky,
And white clouds scudding swiftly, lead the thought
To cheerful lessons by kind season taught.
Nature is full of life ; the grass, the trees,
And soil, enriched by sun, by shower, by breeze ;
Lambs, in the fields, leap in their frolic gay,
And scampering little dogs bark loud at play.

At such a time, when Tom, out in the field,
To guided ploughshare made the hard clay yield,
A sudden thought rose strongly in his brain,
Sudden, though there it long had dormant lain,
But now gained power, the thought should be a
    fact,
And, all at once, he made resolve to act.
Then ploughed as one who would not win a prize,
Nor cared for it, 'twas nothing in his eyes ;
With wandering brain, he only wished to be
At end of work in hand and from it free.
And, when his task was done, he took his pay,
And packed his bundle, and went far away.
Long he had tired of rural life, and now
Hoped in the world to make a brighter show.

No more he'd rise with lark, but take more ease,
No toil distasteful should again displease,
Of work of spirit now his mind was full,
In lively town far from the country dull.
No more in corduroy clad, or moleskin, he,
Dressed in bright cloth, a smarter man would be;
Not once regretted life he'd leave behind,
A wild enthusiasm now filled his mind,
And, as he went, with beating heart, along,
Met Jessie singing a small childish song.
"Oh! little Jess," he said, while shone his eye,
"I'm going to the county-town; good-bye."
"What," said the little girl, "what, Tom? Oh! dear,
Why Jenny says that you can do best here."
"What Jenny says is all as one," said he,
"For I'm resolved that I'll a soldier be,
So, good-bye, Jess." Then went with heart so light
Filled with the thought of martial glory bright,
And soon met Jenny and told his intent.
While Jessie forward on her errand went.

Now little Jessie stopped her little song,
Which she was singing as she walked along,
When near to Tomlin's, and, with anxious look,
And timid, halting step, her way she took,
Then, suddenly ran on, in childish fright,
Hoping to get past and not to be in sight
Of any one; but Bob, her tormentor,
As in such cases happens, soon saw her,

And urged his little legs to greatest height
Of their small speed to overtake her flight,
But she a good start had, and kept her pace,
So him she distanced in this childish race.

Then, at grandfather's house, her message told,
And spoke of Bob, as bad as he was bold.
"Oh! grandfather, Bob Tomlin came, and he——"
"Oh! Bob, yes, he's a bad one, so I see,
And so I say, and so I think him too.
Eh! little Jessie, what's he done to you? .
Did Bobby want to kiss you, eh, my dear?."
And kindly light shone in his blue eyes clear,
His toothless wrinkled mouth in pleasure's smile
Expanded, as he fondly gazed the while
On his granddaughter. Then the little child
Thought she would like some fun; with action wild
She tugged his smock-frock; feeble struggle made
The old man as his grandchild with him played,
He laughed, and coughed, as he the room around
Was dragged, in frolic weak. On common ground
Here age and childhood met, for childhood thought
Itself important that age could be brought
To join in its own sport, while age would fain
Seem, while at child's play, to be young again.

Soon came the old man's daughter and his son
Home from their work; he told of Jessie's fun,
And laughed, and gasped, while tears ran down his face;
Breathless with pleasure after such a chase.

He took his seat, and, when he'd gained his breath,
He told wee Jessie of Cock Robin's death,
And of the sparrow, and, when she had heard,
She said, indignant, "What a naughty bird!"
And then he told her the whole story through,
Although he made one verse for many do,
And gave to some bird credit which was due
Unto some other, nor kept quite in view
The story's thread, that oft the aunt brought back
Incipient wanderings to their proper track.

Oh! little joys, and then come little fears;
But are they little? For, when few in years,
On unformed minds the little fears have told
With as much force as greater when we're old.
Now had she left the joys of grandad's cot,
And to meet Bob might be, perhaps, her lot.
Her childish, dark blue eyes, so large, so clear,
And sweet small mouth, expressed a hidden fear
As she neared Tomlin's house, then, suddenly,
Out at the wicket the dread Bob did fly,
And, as she crossed the lane, he crossed it too,
With straddling legs, with arms extended; who
Could pass such mighty man? Such he appeared
To little Jessie, as about he veered
When she manœuvred to pass by the lad.
But still the little fellow was not bad;
He only wanted fun, and had no thought
Of what great fear small fun has often wrought.

Then, as she stepped aside on to the grass,
He stretched his arms and would not let her pass.
Then drooped her head, and little sulks did show
In her round face, she'd take no notice now.
Then he told of the daring things he'd do,
Which appeared terrible to her. "If you
Do that, you'll catch it, that I'm sure you will."
For though that he so much had teased her, still
She thought it right to warn him of the fate
Which one so dire in threats must aye await.
Then, seeing the impression he had made,
He said that he of no man was afraid;
With little head thrust forward, little eyes
Wide open, as his lips would pouting rise,
In bragging tone spoke of the things which he
Would do. "Yes, Jessie, ah! and you'll just see."

Then, reaching home, she to her mother told
The message sent by grandad, of the bold,
The bad Bob Tomlin. "Why, my little Jess,
Bob is your little sweetheart, one would guess."
"No, mother, no! Oh! that could never be,
He is the rudest boy I e'er did see.
Why, he told me what things he meant to do;
Oh! they were dreadful; I am sure that you
Would not believe them if I told you all.
Why, he said that he meant to go and call
'Hullo, old Blake!' in at the school-room door
When Mr. Blake was teaching; and, what's more,

He said that right through Wilson's field he'd pass;
I said, 'You mustn't, for it's standing grass,
And if, before it's cut, you do go there,
You will annoy him;' he said, 'I don't care;'
He said, 'I don't care if I do annoy.'
Oh! mother, wasn't he a wicked boy?
And who d' you think I met, just by the stile?
Why, Tom, who said he'd make it worth his while
To lead a jollier life than he had led,
For he would be a soldier, so he said."

"What!" cried the mother, "why, what need had he?
Oh! what will Jenny say?" Then turnèd she
Unto her work; the iron, heated through,
Uneasily o'er the starched linen flew,
Guided by her unsteady hand, her skill
Baffled awhile by her too-puzzled will.
She silently thought how, for some time past,
Tom had been changeful, oft had seemed downcast.
Unsettled, had been turning o'er in mind
How he a different line of life might find.
She'd been the first to notice his changed mood,
Which for poor Jenny never boded good.

She heard a footstep, and a neighbour came,
One Mrs. Bates; she handled every name
In all the village and the country round,
And told the latest tidings she had found.
Half heedless heard her friend, in constant fear
Of Tom and Jenny some sad tale she'd hear.

But Mrs. Bates had not yet heard this news,
So questioned, answered, and expressed her views
On things and persons, quite self-satisfied
With all she said, as she would praise or chide.
She suddenly grew serious, looking out
Through th' open doorway. "What's your girl about?"
She said. "Here's Jenny, why she seems quite ill."
When Jenny came all scattered was her will,
As, sinking on a chair, with hollow tone
Of voice, and dry blank face, she said "He's gone."
"Oh! Jenny, is it true?" the mother asked.
Then Jenny, tried to speak, but, overtasked
Her heart, her feelings, could but droop her head,
And violently shook, as the tears sped
Full fast adown her cheeks; to her deep grief
Nor tears nor silence could bring least relief.
Her pain was great, as if that it would tear
Her life away; for when some ponderous care
Crushes the spirit, which it cannot kill,
The body fain would help the spirit's will
By forcèd action, but 'tis all in vain,
Nor writhing frame, sighs, sobs, can break the chain
Which o'er the spirit holds such hard control,
Painful as iron entering the soul,
Till, on the tirèd frame, at length despair
Leaves the dulled spirit 'neath its load of care.
"Yes, mother, he is gone. Oh! why, oh! why
Should he thus leave me? Will he let me die?
Why should he wish to be a soldier? Well
'Twould be for him here 'mid his friends to dwell.

But it has such a hold upon his brain,
This soldiering. He does not know the pain
Which he will suffer, for they say that war
Must soon begin, and he'll be sent afar.
How happy we might both have been! Oh! how
Could he think it was well to leave his plough?
Ah! he was changed; new thoughts were in his head;
And half his peace and all his love were fled.
I could not move him, all that I could say
Was but half listened to, 'twas thrown away.
I was not in his heart; he was so strange;
His thought to glory, battles, e'er would range.
He's gone. Oh! he will never come again!
Why should he careless be to all my pain?"

Said Mrs. Bates, "Why, Jenny, now, don't grieve.
What if your sweatheart leaves you? Let him leave,
And get another." "No," said Jenny, "no."
Then said the mother, "How can you talk so
To one who's troubled? Do you think the heart
Can change, and easily from true love part?"
"Yes, she's in trouble, and I'd help her out.
I never let young men keep me in doubt,
And that's what my first husband always said,
And, when he died, I did another wed.
Why, I would ne'er without a husband be,
No more need you." Then Jenny sighed, "Ah! me,
You don't know what I feel. Oh! Tom; but, no,
He is not mine; ah! to the war he'll go,

And quite forget me; oh! why should it be?
Why should I suffer so? And why should he
Thus be unsettled, when a happy lot
Might here be his, when, in our little cot,
I'd keep his home, and he should have no care?
But this won't please him, he must have some share
In glory, as he calls it. Were he here,
And I his wife, his daily life I'd cheer.
But there is nought but hardship, toil, and grief,
No love unto his work can bring relief,
None but hard men are there, and pain, and strife,
And wounds, perhaps, and even loss of life."
"Jenny," said Mrs. Bates, "now don't you see
It's no use going on so. There's Jim Lee
Just lost his wife, and he will wed again,
Of course he will, the reason is quite plain,
Some one must look to his six children small."
But Jenny, deaf, stared blankly at the wall.
Ah! painful stare; she looked, but nothing saw,
Her sight, her heart, all blank, her feelings raw,
While Mrs. Bates continued, "You don't care
For Jim; well, that's not wise of you; but, there,
I can't make out you girls, that's nowadays,
There's not one of you with the proper ways
To win young fellows, but you mope on one.
Love never upset me, but, if I'd done
The same that girls do now—but they don't know
The proper way, that's why they take on so.
But look about you, now, that's what I say."
And then the world-wise woman went her way.

Poor Jenny grieved and grieved, her woe was deep,
Nought could console her, often would she weep,
As oft her tearless face showed the keen pain
Which on her young, once hopeful, heart had lain.
Nor mother's sympathy could give her ease,
Nor little Jessie's kindly efforts please.
She felt their kindness, felt the kind regard
Of friends, who spoke against Tom's conduct hard.
But she another creature seemed to be,
With broken hope now lost to her was he.

Strange beings, men! Why is it they will stray
From happiness and from true love away?
Why to all quiet joy must they be blind,
When once ambition moves their fickle mind?
Why restless ever, to no object true,
Save when self-glory comes within their view?
Ah! woman's daily work e'er ministers
To the affections, but man's toil e'er stirs
Him to hard deeds, affection must be crushed,
Or, by rough world, his work aside is pushed.

Tom went, but oft there came within his mind
Thoughts of the little maid he'd left behind,
But could not hold within his changing heart.
And, though, in love, he'd played a traitor's part,
In Glory's cruel grasp he was held fast,
And served that hard taskmaster to the last,
And with his heart as well as hand worked he,
No conscript soldier, but a Briton free,

Fought on Crimean hills, at Inkerman,
And met with death while storming the Redan.

Time partially dulled the once sharp pain
Which Jenny suffered. Perhaps, ere Tom was slain,
She might, at times, have thought he had been hard,
And, by degrees, have lessened some regard.
But this is certain, Stephen came, and, lo!
He dried the tears which Tom had caused to flow;
But not at once; his courtship lingered long,
With Jenny still the love for Tom was strong,
But, if it could not die, hope could not live
For ever on what never might arrive.
For all she heard of Tom was from some friend,
No token he to her did ever send.
Kind-hearted Stephen, in his way, was sage,
Though knowledge to his eyes her ample page,
Rich with the stores of time, did ne'er unroll,
He had true knowledge in his humble soul.
For he was wise in roots, and crops, and soil,
Weather, and things pertaining to his toil;
One who in mild ambitions will excel,
Who do small things, and do those small things well;
Not, foiled in great attempts, 'gainst fortune rave,
But make the very most of gifts they have.
So he was trusted, and was e'er employed,
And, quiet in his tastes, his home enjoyed.
She learned to love him, love must sometimes be
Learned, it not always comes spontaneously.

And, if to brilliant Tom her thoughts would rove,
The quiet might of Stephen's gentle love
On her affections gained with slow, sure pace,
And all thought, save for him, away did chase.

'Tis years since I have in that village been,
And it is many miles away, yet e'en
Now, as I think of it, it seemeth near,
That village sweet. Ah! in the memory clear
E'er dwells some scene that nothing can efface,
Nor change, nor sameness; no, nor time, nor place.
The seasons have gone round and made up years,
The grown-up folks are old, the little dears
That played their games, now men and women are,
Some still are there, and some have moved afar.
But still the children play, and seasons veer,
E'er moving, round each new succeeding year.

Prologue to the Working-Man's Tale.

THE Ploughman spoke, "Now, lady, for my part,
I thank you for that tale, aye, from my heart.
'The short and simple annals of the poor,
Their homely joys and destiny obscure,'
As said the scholar, whose warm soul could find
Strong sympathy with poor unlettered hind.
Why, these poor folk it is of nations make
The bulk, and should be honoured for the sake
Of work and good they do, though oft unseen,
For, without them, the great had hardly been."

"Give me your hand, old boy," the Workman said,
"Those very thoughts have oft run through my head.
And I say, give us still our homely joys,
For if one thing there be that me annoys
More than aught else, it is when fellows come
And try to talk us out of house and home,
And make us discontented with our lot,
Instead of happier in it. Why, 'tis not
For every man upward to rise in life;
And, if he can't rise, what's the good of strife?

He'd better make the best of that which he
Possesses, and add to it if there be
The chance, and if he find he has the skill,
And perseverance, intellect, and will,
Which go to make a great man, he'll be one.
If not, why should he, just for others' fun,
Or interest, work, as a tool, on schemes
Which make his lofty hopes mere empty dreams?"

The Merchant spoke. "Ah! in my time," he said,
"The workmen did work, and for it were paid.
But now they clamour for employment they,
Oft vainly, seek. Why, in the present day,
Should there be always such a numerous horde
Of unemployed men? Can't your times afford
To keep all men at work? Why should there be
Hosts of industrious men continually
Forced to be idle? Is't your normal state?
Mind, or to mend you'll find 'twill be too late.
You modern men will have to change your way
Of doing things, or else you'll find each day
Things will get harder, for 'tis hard for all
When hardship does on any section fall.
You do too much, and yet too little do;
You make work, but don't do work, and you rue
Whene'er you think upon the olden days,
And of their work so solid, beyond praise.
And why? Why, workmen then were taught to work,
No man unskilled could 'mid the skilful lurk,

And trades' guilds overlooked all work begun,
And certified its quality when done.
But, moderns, you do things on such a scale,
Machinery doth o'er workmanship prevail,
And you boast quantity, size, number, when
It seems (at least to me) machines kill men.
I mean not bodily, but in their mind.
Is it not so? For e'en you moderns find
Men less learn handicraft than how to tend
Machines which make by thousands, and the end
Is that intelligence and skill must fall,
For want of use, like weakest 'gainst the wall.
And manufactured goods in numbers made,
Oft flimsily, must overstock a trade;
And then, to push them, come the middleman,
The agent, traveller, all those who can
Not do the work themselves, but in one round
Of o'er-excited energy are found.
But, were at work all fingers, heads, and hands,
Instead of dull machinery's cogs and bands,
Less would be made, but more would, sure, be done,
And less excitement would through mankind run.
Instead of making grosses in short space
Of time, and worrying with feverish race
To sell, and quick make others in their place,
And, fearing slack times and men unemployed
If orders come not in to fill the void
Caused by reaction following that too-fast
Production which cannot for ever last;
If, seeking not mere speed, if slow, yet sure,
Were steady, skilful hands, work would endure,

Be longer doing, but be better done,
Employment in more even line would run,
Minds would grow calmer, and each question great
Which heats you moderns into fierce debate
Would be much better met. Calmed minds would cast
Hot feelings far away. But you're so fast,
And yet so slow. Do work that shall endure
To other ages as good work and pure.
Be not like dogs which back and forward run,
Cross and recross their road, yet not like one
Make progress, who'll trudge on from hour to hour,
And end his journey with least waste of power."

"Ah!" said the Workman, with a mighty sigh,
"That's a fine dream, sir. Could we but apply
Ourselves as you say, it would better be,
But we're mere guiders of machinery,
For the most part ; and so, our brains and skill
Are lying fallow, much against our will.
The dignity of labour now is seen
As a mere hanger-on to a machine.
When will Demand demand sound work from men,
And when Supply supply it? When, ah! when?"

"For answer," said the Host, "you long may wait.
So now, I pray, a tale to us narrate.
And, after that, you, Ploughman, tell a tale."
"I will," replied the Ploughman, "without fail.
I told one once in bluff King Harry's reign,
And what I have done I can do again."
"Yes," said the Host, "but 'tis not yet your day,
Wait till the other's done, then say your say."

The Working-Man's Tale.

IT WAS early in the sixteenth century,
When Europe, so distracted in its faith,
Saw men, grieved at corruptions in the Church
(Which they could not purge, nor could bring her back
To pure faith, primitive and Catholic),
Tear themselves from her, and then set up faith
Unapostolic, and of recent growth;
And, 'mid these men, rose others, who set forth
Doctrines more novel, individual,
And making discord in their common cause.
And thus division did division breed.

At last arose a sect, whose creed declared
That to their leaders it had been revealed,
In visions and in dreams divine (for such
Their fancies and their thoughts to them appeared),
That all the world must be anew baptized,

For the baptism, Christ's Church had ever taught
From its beginning, no true baptism was.
This strange, self-certain sect some progress made
In Münster; secret were their meetings first,
But soon their numbers grew, and Catholics
And Protestants, together, took alarm,
And, joining forces, from the city drove
The Anabaptists, so these folks were called.
They soon returned in confidence and zeal,
And did intimidate the Town Council;
And when, by this act, they'd gained great success,
And one bold stroke would bring full victory,
Next day, one of their preachers, furious, ran
Along the street, exclaiming, as he went,
" Repent! Repent! Reform, and be baptized,
Or suffer God's just vengeance!" The hard shock,
Given by the clamorous in exciting times,
Was felt throughout the town. The people flocked
In fear, excitement, thoughtlessness, dismay;
And thus were numbers gained, and they went on
To wider fields of action; for they seized
Cannon and ammunition, next, possessed
The town-hall, summoned then their brethren all,
In the near-lying towns, to come at once
To Münster. "Leave all that you have," they wrote.
" Wives, children, houses, all your loss shall be
Tenfold to you repaid." The richer folks
Left Münster, while the Anabaptists, swift
In numbers pouring in, soon gained such strength,
That they were masters, and possessed the town.

Then one whose utterances they thought divine,
Whom they esteemed a prophet, Matthiesen,
Commandment gave that all, without reserve,
On pain of death, if they dared disobey,
Should bring their goods into one common stock.
The terrified folk gave obedience,
And property of those who'd left the town
Was confiscate.   This done, he ordered next
That all books, save th' Old Testament and New,
Should be thrown in the flames, and in the square,
In front of the cathedral, there were burned
Some twenty thousand florins' worth of books.
With boundless power implicitly obeyed
He thought he was inspired from above,
For, as the city was that time close pressed
(Since Münster's Bishop, thrust forth from his home,
Had gathered forces, and besieged the town)
He gave it out that 'twas to him revealed
He should repulse the enemy, and ran
Fast through the streets, a halberd in his hand,
Exclaiming loudly as he flew along,
" The Father orders me to chase the foe ! "
But he'd no sooner through the town-gate passed
When he was slain.

Dismayèd at his death, the people then
By John of Leyden had their courage roused,
And, with enthusiasm, following him,
They fierce repulsed, with a heavy loss,
The assault of the besiegers on the town.

John, placed in power, then cast a longing eye
Upon the widow of slain Matthiesen,
For she a very handsome woman was;
A prophet might a prophet's widow wed;
He married her. Soon afterwards he told
Great revelation had been made to him
Concerning marriage, and the preachers then,
For three days in succession, taught their flocks
That men should have plurality of wives.

Their John, their prophet, formerly had been
A tailor's journeyman; he, now so great,
Appointed twelve, chosen from the faithful ones,
To lead the flock; ancients of Israel.
Yet oft he thought that there must be a king;
As often thought that he must be that king;
Afflicted, agitated by such thought,
Prayed that he might be spared from kingly care,
Since he too humble was for such a lot;
But, if that otherwise it should be willed,
Might it but be vouchsafed that prophets true,
Worthy of faith, should show that 'twas ordained
By power on high that he should be the king.
Yet never spoke his thought to any one,
But communed with himself and held his peace,
Till, suddenly, a prophet new appeared,
Who told the people it had been revealed
To him that John of Leyden was to rule
O'er all the earth, and sit on David's throne
Till God should come and claim that throne from him.

Then the twelve ancients did their power resign,
And John of Leyden was proclaimèd king.

Oh! man of lowly birth on sudden raised
To kingly power, and ruling over those
Whose goods were held in common, now drew forth
From common lot to keep his kingly state;
His prophet-given kingly state he deemed.
Oh! thought dwelt on to kill all other thoughts,
And make folks hemmed-in in a narrow siege
Believe that they're the kingdom of the world.
Ah! while the siege did press, and the poor folks
Could scarce get food, he held a royal court,
And, dressed in rich robes covered o'er with gold,
With silver ornaments from churches ta'en,
Sat in great splendour, 'mid his many wives.
Ofttimes, in state, the city he'd parade,
Riding a horse adorned with cloth of gold,
At his right hand a splendidly dressed page
Carried a Bible, and a triple crown
Surmounted by a globe, and that transfixed
By two bright swords, a gold and silver one,
And, 'twixt them, a small cross, thereon inscribed
"A king of justice over all the world;"
And, on his left, there went another page
Who carried in his hand a naked sword.
And, in such state, he would give audience
To those who'd business with him, and who, when
They near approached, must thrice prostrate themselves,
Ere they had hearing.

                        One day, in the square,
Four thousand people sat down to a meal;
Their king, his wives, and servants of his house
Waited upon them, and, when all had fed,
They then engaged in what was mockery
Of the most solemn Supper of the Lord.

Strange city! Where each man had many wives,
Where e'en young girls of twelve were forced to wed;
And yet whose people, oft in want of food,
Would sometimes feed on bodies of the slain.
Still, by such feeling strong were they possessed,
That they believed their John of Leyden was
A prophet sent from God, and that, in time,
He should the whole world rule, as minister
To carry out what Scripture had foretold.
And he himself believed that he was sent
Upon a mission which was working out
The will of God; and, while the poor folk starved,
And gave their all into a common fund,
He kept a state and grandeur which he thought
Were rightly his; and though, meanwhile, he ruled
His people with the sternest despotism,
The despotism that doth enslave the will,
He left them to their passions uncontrolled,
Thus roused their fury to exalt his cause,
While they, and all they had, belonged to him.

At last the city by assault was ta'en,
After resistance obstinate, and with

A frightful slaughter of these misled men.
And John of Leyden, and, along with him,
His vicar and lieutenant, all were seized,
And placed in prison, where they justified
All they had done by saying that their reign
Was that same kingdom Scripture had foretold;
Nor could believe (although their cause destroyed
Had shown such prophecies they'd had were false)
That they were wrong, except in few small points
Quite immaterial to the general cause.
Soon these three men, in manner barbarous,
Were executed in the public view.

Oh! strange enthusiasm which fiercely urged
Oppressors and oppressed, that both believed
Their cause was God's; bearing all kinds of pain,
Believing that, ere long, o'er all the world
There should be nought but that which they believed;
Indulging in coarse passions, thus inflamed
In mind and body, taking, willingly,
Fancy or wish for revelation true.
God save us from false prophets and false Christs.

The Ploughman's Tale.

SIRS, it befel, that, once upon a day,
    In Southwark, at the Tabard as I lay;
    Excuse me, governor, that here I took,
    To get a start, a leaf out of your book;
    Although you'll say that it is not a leaf,
    'Tis scarce two lines; that's true; but, to be brief,
Two lines of yours the quality express
That's found in a whole leaf whose force is less.
Why now, this cockney, early in the day,
In a brown study riding on the way,
Mused much on quantity and quality,
And size, weight, worth, and such-like things that be.
And I know he was right; how oft I've found
The difference there is in plots of ground.
A hyde of some land's worth no more to plough
Than half an acre somewhere else, I vow.
"Man," cried the Host, "do sink the plough and flail;
D'ye call that brief? Come, go on with your tale."
Ah! but I know, for I've ploughed many a field,
And know not always best ploughed brings best yield;

That's no excuse, though, not to plough it well ;
But soil is soil, as I can fairly tell.
For I was in the country born and grown,
Though once I did come up to London town,
And crossed the bridge and into Southwark went,
Before I took my journey into Kent,
And there I put up at the Tabard Inn.
Now, sirs, I'm ready ; now I will begin.

As I sat in the room, in came a wight
Was staying there, I don't think he was bright,
But he asked me if I had seen the cat,
I told him " No," and then he said that that
Confirmed his worst fears ; well, I asked him then
What fears he had. He wa'n't like other men
Who answer straight, for he looked up and down,
And drew a long breath, and his wit seemed flown,
And his eyes looked as if that they could stray
And see what wasn't there, but miles away.
Said he, " That cat's a witch, and so, by you
Unseen, it came, and vanished from view."
" Why, man," said I, " now, don't talk in that key,
It might have been here, though unseen by me,
For I've been sitting o'er this pot of ale ;
Come, take a drink ; don't let your courage quail
At thought of witches, there are none about."
" Alas !" said he, " this is an age of doubt,"-
And turned his eyes up, and seemed really grieved
That others were not like himself deceived.

He seemed to have a very mortal fear
Of witches, and of ghosts, and all things queer,
And all he'd heard of what could work a charm,
And dreaded everything that could do harm,
But had no confidence in anything
Could happiness, or peace, or pleasure bring.
Sudden he said, " From Warwickshire I've come,
And thence through Oxfordshire took the road home,
And, 'twixt those counties, near the Edge Hill range,
I saw some groups of stones that were most strange ;
The rustics told me all their history."
And here I'll tell you what he told to me.

At night Canidia stood
Within the wood.
The darkness all around
Was so profound
That nought was seen
Of tree or thicket green,
Nought seen but darkness unalloy'd,
Nought but a gloomy huge black void.

Was she on earth? Was she in air?
Or 'neath the earth, in regions where
Strange beings dwell, we should not fear?
Strange beings we too often fear,
Because (so strong their power drear)
Weak faith, by them assail'd,
Hath often in their presence quail'd.
She trod on earth, though earth did seem
As if to her 'twere but a dream.

Such influence possessèd she,
She more than mortal seem'd to be.
Though of the earth, her senses all
By beings strange so held in thrall,
Earth seem'd mere shadow, and the air
A solid realm where spirits rare,
Unseen, unheard, yet with her mind
Affianced, strong as sense could bind.
Canidia some moments there
   Waited and listened, but no sound
Of voice, upon the murky air,
   Was borne from anywhere around.
Then onward she, with toiling footsteps, went
Through tangled undergrowth, which bent
Beneath her stumbling tread. Slow was her pace,
Slender tree-sprays, unseen, oft swept her face;
And bramble branches, in her track,
Caught in her dress and held it back,
That oft she was compelled to halt till she
Had from their thorny clutch her skirt set free;
Then, uttering foul oath, would onward pass.
The silent viper wriggled through the grass,
The bat flew round in distant noiseless flight,
   Or, coming near, would bring
   The hurried sound of swiftly flapping wing;
And frogs' rough croak rose through the deadly night.

She saw a grisly light upon the ground,
   And knew 'twas but the surface cool
   Of stagnant marshy pool;
'Twas almost dark as the grim blackness round;

Scarce was its outline seen, so blended 'twas
With sodden'd weed, rank sedgy grass;
So faint it shone, 'twas merely darkness made
But something weaker than its deepest shade.
By the foul pool in the deep wood
All motionless she silent stood,
And waited for some omen good.
Oh! good? ah! me, but it was harm
She wished; for she'd prepared a charm,
A magic charm, and sought to know
How she might farthest go
In working ill, and raise a yell
Of joy from fiends in deepest hell.

She long into the pool intently gazed,
At last her falling hope was raised,
For she could see
(And miles below the pool it seemed to be)
A lurid flame of ruddy fire,
First slow, then swiftly, mounting higher
Until it to the surface came,
When instant disappeared the flame.
Then came a loud strange voice, painful and slow,
Exclaiming dismally: "Canidia, go,
Work out the charm, the magic meshes twine,
And all, in thirteen days, shall then be thine."

Then from the pool Canidia turned,
For she from those strange words had learned
That which she wished to know; they brought
Reply to her unuttered thought.

Then slowly dawn'd on her a sense
Of life within the lone wood dense.
She voices heard, and whispering,
And laughter which no thought of joy could bring,
Light sounds of many hurrying feet,
   Of one huge being's heavy tread,
   Sound of the voices of the dead,
Known in their life, who her by name would greet ;
Rustling garments touched her, fluttering by,
   Hands would stroke her face ; in air
Were cries both loud and faint, below, on high,
   Of mirth, of foulness, sadness, and despair.
And as she heard, her whole mind, heart, and soul
Lived, breathed, conspired with these beings foul.

At length she left the haunted wood,
And on the rugged heath she stood,
Fatigue of body did succeed
To eager thought, from thought now freed.
She slowly, slowly crossed the heath,
With lagging step, with labouring breath,
Then gained her home,
   Yet scarce could sleep,
For through her mind there still would roam
   Wild thoughts of mischief deep.
Though now assured that mischief would be done,
Her yet uncalmèd mind on thoughts of it would run.

Day after day she carefully looked o'er
Her ill-acquired store

Of things she used for magic rite,
Herbs culled in darksome noon of night,
Gifts gained by the threat of her evil eye,
And spoils torn from the dead in years gone by.
With these she brewed a powerful broth, so vile
That, hurled aloft, 'twould so the air defile,
That she to any form she wish'd could doom
All who within its influence might come.

Then dawned a day, with brilliant sunny morn,
Yet such a day, it was, by noontide, shorn
Of brilliancy, for, though the sun still shone,
Yet brightness all from it was gone.
Mist dulled the once blue sky, the now-dimmed sun
Any, with eye unhurt, might gaze upon,
So faint it shone in grey thick heated air;
    And all the scene so weird
    Unto the sight appeared
Unreal seemed the landscape fair.
Sky seemed as solid as the earth,
    Earth seemed as airy as the sky,
Nor light nor shadow had its worth
    Of brightness or opacity;
So dim the light, so weak the shade,
That faintness did all things pervade.

Came an army, led by a king,
Who would into subjection bring
The neighbouring kingdom, which, o'erthrown,
England he hoped to make his own.

Slowly they toiled across the heath,
With heated body and with panting breath,
With spirit dulled by the heavy day,
And thought of their homes so far away,
And a lurking doubt as to victory,
They were almost ripe for mutiny.
Afar from them the peasants fled.
Canidia, all free from dread,
Yet at a distance, watched to see
Those who would soon her victims be.
Strange whisperings in her ear
Told her the time was near,
Strange beings unseen at her side
Did every footstep guide.
She knew by each strange sign
That every influence malign
Was working now with furious might,
Anon she cackled with delight,
Throbbing with excitement, strained
   Her resolution to such height
That it should strongest act; she'd gained
   So much, e'en now, some blight
Might spoil her work at last,
And all her mighty preparation blast.
But e'en the very air did seem
To speak to her, as, in some painful dream,
We know things which we are not told;
And now she seemed now hot, now cold,
Shaken with excitement great,
Resolved on deed of deadly hate.

She feared, she hoped, she doubted, joyed;
Pleasure with despair alloyed
Was hers; some chance might yet o'erthrow
    Her plot, if not, the time was now at hand
When king and army she'd lay low,
    For nothing mortal could her spell withstand.

And she watched, with a joy both wicked and sweet,
As she heard the tramp of their sandalled feet,
And over the hill-top saw banner and spear
Rising higher, and coming each moment anear;
Saw the helmets, and soon came the troops into sight,
As the shoulder they cleared of the round lofty height,
Saw their armour of bronze with its curious design
Of well-hammered boss and of stiff curving line,
Saw the sword or the spear which each warrior bore,
And the torques and the bracelets the bold leaders wore,
Saw them march on, and sudden halt,
    And heard the words their king
Addressed to them, "Soon the assault
    We'll make, and it shall certain victory bring.
Here pitch your tents, brave lads, alone I'll go
To the hill's edge, and scan our doomèd foe."

"What could that mean?" Five of his knights did ask
Each other. They were weary of their task.
Each for promotion had his own design,
And would himself incline
To any plot, or plot within a plot.
Each wished to change his lot,

THE PLOUGHMAN'S TALE.

Wished up to higher rank to fly,
And saw that wish plain in his fellow's eye.
Soon as the troops began to pitch
Their tents, and dig defending ditch,
From them these rebel knights withdrew,
And, at some furlong's distance, threw
Their thoughts together, whispering,
With heads near touching, plots against their king,
Who slowly rode on toward the hill-top high,
Thinking of conquest, he now sure, was nigh.

THE SOLDIERS.

Free soldiers now are we,
To-morrow slaves may be ;
Though joined together a foe to fight,
Yet we find, in our despite,
That faction is setting us now by the ear ;
   If they who lead
   Turn thought into deed,
Our valour will soon be no better than fear.
For discord's fell power full often has wrought
Greater prize for a foe than a battle well fought.
But each, in the fight, will e'en do his best,
And our leaders, forsooth, must settle the rest.
Why should we care for what cause we fight ?
If it be for the wrong, if it be for the right ?
While we get pay, ah ! and plunder, and joy
Of the rush of the battle, what care can annoy ?

THE FIVE WHISPERING KNIGHTS.

FIRST KNIGHT.

How fast the world seems going down,
For now all kind of sense is flown;
New-fangled things are new upsprung,
And nothing's as when I was young.
For it used to be thought, in my day,
That a man, when he'd nothing to say,
Should be silent. It now is the thing
For every dull blockhead to bring
The weight of his brains
To tell you the pains
That he's taken to learn, oh! so very much less
Than most folks at once at a mere glance could guess.

SECOND KNIGHT.

What are thy griefs compared with mine?
I to rebellion never did incline.
What can I do, with my estate
All mortgaged, and my castle great
In bad repair, while children, wife
Are put to shifts to keep up life?
I bargained with my king for gold
When his design to me he told;
At once the sum he paid to me
Was spent on my necessity,
And what I must have, in my need,
I seek by risky rebel deed.

THIRD KNIGHT.

Brave friends, complain not, make me king,
    And I'll redress each wrong;
Old knight, old times I back will bring;
    And thou, friend, not for long
Shall want thy noble self oppress,
I with good fortune thee will bless
When this base tyrant is thrown down,
And on my head is placed the crown.
And you, young knights, but act with me,
And guerdon rich shall yours soon be.

FOURTH KNIGHT.

Eh! What? I'm just as good as thou;
At least—well, I'll explain—but now,
Methinks, 'twere better to pretend
We're for the king, and, in the end—
I mean, e'en now, we'll seem to be
All serving him, and, after we
Have pulled him down, and when that I
Am king—ah! no; the reason why
I put it thus, I mean, when we
Have gained our end, we'll then agree
To find what's best we each can gain.
I think that now I've put it plain.

FIFTH KNIGHT.

Well, I am in for what I like;
For any jolly cause I'll strike;

Ah! In the wars with glee I've fought,
Where girls, all helpless, oft I've caught.
For king I neither care nor think,
So I've good share of fun and drink;
I'm always very much amused
When I see anything confused,
So, as our king thus high has flown,
I'll laugh to see him tumbled down.

THE KING.

But few more steps, and I shall be
Where I my foeman's walls can see;
Then, when, for him, 'twill be too late
To call his troops, I'll seal his fate;
For a good augury told me
I'd vanquish every enemy.
The moment now is close at hand
When I shall gain my foeman's land,
All other realms will be my due
Soon as his citadel I view,
For if Long Compton I can see,
King of England I shall be.

The sunny morn drooped to a hazy noon,
    The hazy noon fainted in gloomy eve.
When, full of languor, nature seemed to swoon,
    The heavy air began itself to weave
Into fierce clouds that slowly upward rise,
As thunders muttered in the distant skies.

The Ploughman's Tale.

Then on Canidia swiftly went,
With striding step, with body bent,
With head held low, with gleaming eye
Fixed on the king, she now drew nigh.
She bore a vase which held the potion strong
Brewed by herself for this great deed of wrong,
She breathless stood, intent to fling
It o'er the king.
Should he but few more paces tread,
And view his foeman's town, then fled
Would be the time to work the spell.
Paused she one moment, then, with venom fell,
And rapid action fierce, she swung on high
The vase, and from its mouth did fly
The potion vile, which quickly spread in air,
And (guided by some demon power rare)
Smote king, knights, army, all,
And on them did with death-stroke fall,
For, without sigh, or cry, or moan,
They, in an instant, all were changed to stone.
There, since that hour, they stand upon the ground.
   E'en where they stood
   When life was good,
   E'en there they fell
   When worked the spell,
And, shapeless blocks, they strew the fields around.

" Well, sir," I said unto him when he'd done,
" I don't like such tales ; I prefer some fun,

Or something nice, or tale of lovers' fate,
But this is nothing but a tale of hate."
"Yes, but," he said, "can't you see what I mean?
I tell you of the very things I've seen.
And—there you are—of course I need not say
Another word, the proof's as clear as day."
"Don't talk like that," said I, "but clear your brains,
And search out brighter matters, and the grains
Of sense, that's if you have them, will increase,
And bring you happiness, and pleasant peace."

"Well," said the Host, "he took not your advice.
In these strange matters he became more nice,
And more and more so, though we laughed at him
As solemnly he'd speak of some dull whim,
Of haunted houses, of unlucky sign,
Of things bewitched, of influence malign
Upon him cast; sometimes he'd say the house,
He lived in, some bad influence would rouse,
And he must move to some place where the spell,
Bereft of favouring influence, could not tell.
We tried to cure him of these thoughts; in vain;
For they'd ta'en such a hold upon his brain,
That he became a mystic solemn bore.
How he obtained his living—well, that's more
Than I can tell, or any of his friends,
Or how he managed to make meet both ends.
But this we knew, and joyfully would own,
He never came to beg for any loan."

Prologue to the Author's Tale.

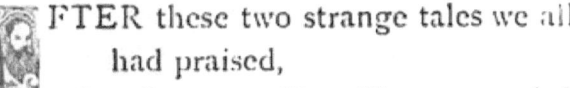

AFTER these two strange tales we all
    had praised,
I rode up to Dan Chaucer, and I
    raised
My hat, and asked of him if, kindly,
    he
Would tell me the best way to——. Suddenly
The Host cried out, "There's one left; hi! you there,
In modern dress, who barbarous trousers wear,
Like ancient Briton, Gaul, or Scythian dread,
Tell us a tale." "Now, pray, Sir Host," I said,
"Don't joke my dress: 'tis ugly, I must say,
Compared with yours, but yours first 'gan to stray,
Toward fantasy, away from elegance,
Yours took the first step in a downward dance.
With dress went architecture, hand in hand,
Down, though each oft would try to make a stand;
In vain. In your days, Perpendicular
Began, and soon had spread itself afar,
And Gothic drooped, next died; then Renaissance,
With Gothic steps went through a Classic dance,
Till, grown quite weary, Taste went fast asleep,
And o'er her sleepiness we needs must weep,
For we poor moderns, with our o'ergrown towns,
Live where soul-killing Dulness on us frowns.

"The simple, graceful, mediæval dress
Shewed, in your day, the first sign of distress;
For it was whimsical; it might be quaint,
But all its grace was weak, and no restraint
Was held on form; soon, then, rank wildness grew,
And dress in every kind of strange shape flew;
And as, by mixing many a colour bright,
You'll make a new one that's as dull as night,
So Fashion's antics did at length compress
Themselves into our shapeless modern dress.
But "Place aux Dames!" as Frederick Fairholt
    says,
Or quotes, and we've seen, in these latter days,
Most charming ladies' dresses, ah! the fair
Set us a good example, for compare
Their ugly dress worn forty years ago
With what to-day makes such a pretty show,
Then think of our poor dress, as dull as when
Grandfathers wore the same; ah! tasteless men!"

"Well," said the Host, "put shoulder to the wheel,
You modern men, if bad taste's pinch you feel.
For you're so clever, all you modern lads,
With your steam-engines and your ironclads,
Your railways, cutting up the beauteous vales,
Your printing-presses, and the balmy gales
Of what you call intelligence, your mood
For bettering nature, artificial food,
Your gunpowder, your wonderful fire-arms,
Which give such splendid zest to war's alarms,

The big things that you build and then pull down,
The great streets that you make in every town.
You do great things in this great generation,
Wholesale, and retail, and for exportation.
   "Well, you have said, and I did never hear
One talk to me as you have talked. What cheer
Can you provide, if any? To reprove
You, I'll set you a theme. Tell us of love."

"Yes, love," they murmured, "that's a subject sweet."
"Not always," said I. "Stay," said Host, "complete
Your tale and comments both, but don't begin
To waste your arguments; go in and win."

The Author's Tale.

OVE is a—no, that's not what I mean.
Love is the—that's just as bad, I ween.
Love is—it is—of course, as all can tell,
It is—love is—yes, yes, go on, well, well.
Love is—well, everybody knows what 'tis,
Yet (all will, sure, agree) a hard task this
To try to tell what others don't define,
Although of love they've written many a line.
One says that "we forget," then says, "no, no;"
Strange contradiction; yet, 'tis even so.
Love is a power, though so very slight;
Invisible, well seen; weak, full of might;
So hidden, evident; such pain, such balm;
A joy, a woe; a madness, and a calm.

Why, this is rambling. Surely, none should rove
Whene'er they'd write, or think, or speak, of love.
Of love we glibly talk as of the sun,
The unfailing source of light, whose course is run,

Day after day, in majesty immense,
Yet oft, unseen by us, our mortal sense
Saith that he shineth not, when but some cloud
Dims not his lustre, but our sense doth shroud;
With changing weather we his brightness blame,
His, which still shines with splendour e'er the same.
E'en so with love, 'tis one true perfect light,
Oft, for our sins, all hidden from our sight,
Oft, through our folly, partially disclosed,
Oft blamed by those who have its course opposed,
Cursed as a source of woe by those in pain
Of life that's wrecked, or who have loved in vain,
With quiet rapture held as thing most dear
By those few loving without doubt or fear.
Oh! love, thou'rt constant, ever thou'rt the same,
And, when we doubt it, we've ourselves to blame;
Our passions, interests, thoughts, make base alloy
With love's pure gold, which they would fain destroy.
Love e'er exists, but, coming from above,
Blends not with dross which thinks itself is love.

When England's monarch, fallen from his estate,
Condemned, imprisoned, did his death await,
" This tell my wife," he of his child besought,
" I've ne'er to her been false, even in thought."
Strange speech, strong words, but who their truth could
    doubt?
He knew his course of life would soon run out,
He had no hope to win the ringing cheer
Of partisans who'd favourably hear,

For round were foes who looked on him as sent,
A criminal, unto just punishment.
Calmly he looked toward dread eternity,
To which we ever tend, for him 'twas nigh;
In but few days he'd be beyond the reach
Of mortal joy or ill.   Could we doubt speech
At such time uttered? "Not false, e'en in thought."
It seems beyond belief that feeling fraught
With such intense, unbroken, fervent love
Could e'er be found away from realms above.

Some say that love inspires, that it can make;
And this, for an example, they will take.
A blacksmith, working for his daily gains,
While forging horse-shoes, forging bolts and chains,
Or taking a horse-hoof upon his knee,
And nailing on a shoe, will suddenly
Turn from his blacksmith work, take up a brush,
Into a painter's studio will rush,
And work so hard, and with such right-aimed will,
That in short time he gains a master's skill.
For one fair maid hath so inspired his love
That, for her sake, he will right worthy prove
To be her husband, he'll do some great deed,
Will paint a picture, from the forge be freed.
And thus love made a painter from a smith;
So goes the story; and if it were with
The hope of love he did to painting turn,
Painting was not so hard for him to learn

As might appear. He was a blacksmith, true,
But no mere horse-shoe maker. Well he knew
How, on the anvil, to express art's soul,
In iron bend the graceful Gothic scroll,
Form light fantastic leaves, and satyrs free,
And bold knight, challenging, armed cap-a-pie ;
Beauteous design, wrought with a master's touch,
To turn from this to painting not so much
As seems when blacksmith's named ; 'twas but to move
From one art to another, and 'twas love
Which caused the change, but not the genius rare
Which made the paint or iron speak. Howe'er,
Let us be pleased his love became his wife,
And trust that they two led a happy life.

Love does not make ; it oft intensifies ;
A man's own character with love ne'er dies ;
It may be deepened. If he good man be
His goodness gains, through love, intensity.
But, if a man be bad, we often find,
Wishing for woman's love, his wicked mind
May become worse. And if that he be wise
His wisdom gains more light from two bright eyes.
But if, unwise, ne'er taught in wisdom's school,
He fall in love, he's then a bigger fool.
Some say that all are fools when they're in love;
Some, that it levels all ; some, from above
It comes to raise our being to its height.
No doubt 'tis so, but then, love's flame so bright,

Seen through the smoked glass of our narrow cares,
But as a paltry glimmering light appears;
A disappointment, hope, a joy, a woe,
In all these forms love unto us doth show.
Warped by our fate, we've but distorted view
Of love's great self, so constant, bright, and true.

Joe, out one day, and wandering through the street,
Sal, from her work returning, chanced to meet.
And what of that? Why little, yet 'twas much,
'Twas everything, for, oh! their love was such,
And at first sight, and irresistible,
That if not wisely, yet they loved too well.
'Twas boundless love, o'erpowering, undisguised,
Such as should be by all true lovers prized;
For 'twas not born of gold, and so, was pure,
And, free from wealth-disturbing thoughts, secure;
Nor was it an alliance, where one sees
An union made between two families,
Where the affections play a second's part,
And heartless matters are helped by the heart;
Nor did diplomacy's poor keenness move
To gain some point by making feint with love.
But Joe and Sal rejoiced that there should be
No wealth for them, it left their hearts quite free,
Not harassed by base thoughts of keeping pace
With rich relations in life's breathless race;
Nor ever thought they of mere match, or who,
Opposing, might their happiness undo;

No false appearance, and no pride beset
Their love, to weaken it with vain regret,
But, all unhampered, it was free, 'twas strong,
And joyous went from day to day along,
Heedless of care, from thought of future free,
Happy in self, pure, true, fond, kind, ah! me;
But why this sigh? When love, by wile untaught,
Stands isolated from all worldly thought,
Why should its very freedom, carelessness,
So often be the gateway of distress?

Oh! injudicious weddings of the poor,
Which to the wolf will open wide the door,
And, where mere poverty at first is found,
So oft make want and misery abound.
Where poverty comes in at door, they say,
Love through the open window flies away.
While folks e'en penniless will married be,
And breed hereditary misery,
While round their children prowl, in their distress,
The vile thief-trainer and the procuress.
'Tis sad that earth's love is embarrassed so
That the poor lowly it will still keep low,
That if kind answer to its call they give
In helpless misery they e'er must live.

Now Charles, who was the young son of a lord,
Had little means, and so, could but afford
Whatever a lieutenant's pay could buy,
Which was not much for one of lineage high.

When married folks would laughingly declare
He, bachelor, was free from any care,
They little knew the pain that ever weighed
On Charles's heart, in barrack, on parade,
Alone, in company, or e'en when he
By his belovèd Julia's side might be.
Full well he knew her love, but knew he dared
Not marry, if for happiness he cared.
They must be wretched, doomed to poverty,
With all its painful shifts and drudgery,
For, if they trusted chance, and did but stoop
In life a little, how low might they droop
As life wore on! No, he would seek some friend,
And, with good work, he would his fortune mend.

Friend after friend gave no encouragement.
One thought that Charles's time was idly spent,
And Charles unfit for work; another said
Had Charles but called the day before, instead
Of him he'd sent to some post lucrative,
That very post he unto Charles would give.
One didn't know, while others wouldn't move,
Some couldn't act, but every one did prove
To Charles, what he could hardly understand,
How hard it is to seize what's close at hand.
And Time dragged slowly on, and swiftly flew,
For these two things Time both at once can do,
And much they tasted of that Hope deferred
Which makes the heart sick, while their being, stirred

With love intense, had lost its all of peace,
While Charles's income never did increase.
All that he did was baffled by some blight.
When, in a war, he acted well in fight,
A wretched wound stopped chance of bright career,
And no promotion did his efforts cheer,
And, the war over, ere his wound was healed,
He had no further chance of fame in field.
Again at home, nought did his efforts bless,
In all his trials he met with no success.

How oft he wished to set his Julia free,
As oft reproved the wish, but felt that she
Wasted her life, yet she ne'er thought it waste,
To other lover she could never haste;
For she loved Charles, and wished to be his wife,
And, if that might not be, she felt through life
She ne'er could love again, and her true heart,
Unchanging, from her love should never part.
His happiness was unto him a care,
He knew he must not wed that girl so fair;
Yet she was all his joy; who could express
The harmony of face, form, manner, dress,
Which charmed him so, which made that beauteous
    prize
As beauteous to his heart as to his eyes?
Her finished taste and polished manners kind
Came from a cultivated heart and mind,
Her sweet voice spoke the words which e'er exprest
The gentle feelings of a loving breast,

And every word she used seemed ever fraught
With sense responsive to his inmost thought.
Oh! she was everything he'd e'er desired
To find in loving wife, his heart was fired,
She seemed as almost more than his ideal,
His thoughts, ambition, must become more real,
His higher nature rise to greater height,
That he be worthy of such maiden bright.
And he was loved by such an one! Yet dared
Not wed her, if he for her welfare cared.
So, when alone, his thoughts were full of gloom,
Life all so fair, yet seemed dark as the tomb,
Nought came to help him from his dull distress,
All was so bright, yet all was hollowness;
Some fair blue sky, all free from clouds or showers,
We joy to watch, yet know can ne'er be ours.

He with his regiment was to India sent,
And there, the clime's fell power untiring went
Against his health, and cruel progress made,
And he in dangerous illness low was laid.
His end was near, and he, with sorrow rife,
To the kind chaplain told his love, his life.
"'Tis sad," he said, "in this world's wilderness,
To love and be beloved, and ne'er possess;
Aye to be parted, ne'er to reunite,
And e'en to die far from the loved one's sight.
But send to her, far, far across the sea,
Those little gifts of old she gave to me,

And tell her that I loved her to the last;
And, oh! if selfish thought has e'er o'ercast
My love, ask not forgiveness; for her love,
So pure, so true, will in her heart e'er move
The gentlest feeling, when my life shall be
Yielded to Him Who gave it unto me."

And she received his gifts and message fond.
For her was now no joy, but hope, beyond
This world that she in realm of love might stray,
Where light e'er shines, and tears are wiped away;
Where love rests not on any being who
May pass away; but whatsoe'er was true
And good in Charles, and love she had for him,
Should there exist, not with earth's troubles dim,
But shining with true glory, ne'er to fail,
Where perfect love doth everywhere prevail.

Come, let me turn to something that's not sad;
Sure, talk of love should always make us glad.
Well, Tom and Martha in one shop did serve,
From business duties they did never swerve,
Keen, shrewd, and practical, thought everything
That did exist, grist to the mill should bring.
If sentiment they had, it never showed,
Though sentiment's existence they allowed
In those who told them 'twas a glorious prize,
So they said "Yes," for they were worldly-wise.
And, if they loved, what kind of love did bless
These two? Was it an eye to business?

Each, with quick insight, could in other see
A partner who'd in life of value be.
Tom, twenty-one, started a little trade,
At which, 'twas said, he scarce a living made,
Yet, in short time, he told her that his life
Could never prosper while he had no wife.
This was their moment of most sentiment,
When he asked for, and she did give, consent.
Were they romancers, with such poor look-out
To marry? No; to work they set about,
Looked well to everything, ne'er lost a chance,
And fortune kind did on their efforts glance.
Their business throve, and it throve quickly too,
Till to a large establishment it grew,
From low beginning it had risen high;
And then they reared a numerous family,
With muscles good, complexions clear and bright,
And sturdy health, all sleeping well at night.
Then, in his later years, when things improved,
He'd sometimes tell how in his youth he'd loved,
Not like young people now, who love for gold,
But with a passion reckless, strong, and bold;
But found, though he'd been young, full of romance,
The great thing, after all, was the main chance.

Love should be free. Why came pale want to Joe,
Who'd love, but wanted gold? And why should
    woe
Come upon Charles, when love his heart did move,
Who, wanting gold, could never wed his love?

And why should Tom and Martha lightly speak
Of love, as if 'twere but for beings weak?
There is no doubt that Joe, and Charles, and Tom,
Sal, Julia, Martha, in love's martyrdom
Had never suffered, that is, if they could
In everything have acted as they would.
Joe had been happy to the end of life,
Charles ever happy with a loving wife;
Joe had love's impulse, its devotion Charles,
And both of them provoked mean envious snarls
Well known to those who've heard them. Tom, therefore,
Would not o'er sentiment his fate deplore,
So he loved with his mind as much as heart,
Played sensible more than romantic part.
But, 'midst these three, how second-rate was bliss,
Each one a something of true love did miss,
And what great waste of happiness was here,
Where love, chained up, was harassed by vile fear.

Well, this is not a tale, I think;
No chain, but many a scattered link;
But I could show a few links more,
If you would care to look them o'er.
For I could tell of ugly Dick,
Whom beauteous Rose cut to the quick
By her refusal short and plain,
Which caused poor Dick ne'er love again;
Of uglier Bob, who, one fine day,
Stole beauteous Rose's heart away.

Or I might tell how lovely Sue
Could not bring handsome Hal to woo,
While little Nan, whom men called plain,
Big handsome Hal's great heart did gain,
And he a doting husband proved,
All wondering why it was he loved;
Of rustic Phillis, whom the squire
Loved with a hot and fond desire,
And had not married, but that she
Ne'er into sin beguiled would be;
Then, as he thought who was his mate,
His love for her soon changed to hate,
Quite careless as to how she fared,
The while her gentle heart but cared
To make him happy, and, when came
His cruelty, herself she'd blame;
Or I might tell of merry Loo,
Of jovial Fred, who ten did woo
Before on one his heart could fall,
Then, after, said he'd loved them all,
And Loo would say she did believe;
But was she laughing in her sleeve?
I'd tell of Tom, and Dick, and Harry,
I'd tell of Poll, and Bet, and Carrie,
I'd tell of Jack, I'd tell of Jill,
Of black-eyed Susan and of Bill,
I'd tell of A, and B, and C,
And D, and F, and likewise E,
Of those who rhyme, and those who don't,
Of those who will love, those who won't,

But do at last, and, though bereft
Of resolution they have left,
At once will praise, instead of chide
Their resolution set aside.

Sadly the poet sings of him who cursed
   The social wants that sin against youth's strength.
If oft, of such, the woes should be rehearsed,
   What painful tale, ah! and of painful length.
What tale of memories, fondly stored in mind,
Of happy meetings, and of faces kind,
Of shock at parting, of the life so dull
Succeeding to it, while the heart all full,
Amidst its gloom, of memories so bright,
Like thoughts of sunny days in dead of night,
Yearns, hopes, despairs, in one, filled with unrest,
Its thought so bright with dreary fact opprest.

This is no tale. A tale I cannot tell
Of love. Well, is it better, worse, or well,
Or ill? For when a tale of love I'd find
Only examples come into my mind
Of love, a thing scarce palpable, yet real,
Seen variously, still, every one's ideal.
The reckless poor seek it, nor count the cost,
To thoughtful, wanting means, it oft is lost,
Those with small means which grow, the worldly-wise,
With less love satisfied make compromise.

Yet love, in all these cases, is the same,
And all for it have equal lofty aim.
Love, its own self, is one unbroken light,
Its rays alone descend to our poor sight.
Our lot, our sins, our weakness, and our cares
War all against it, ill with us it fares.
These could we cast aside, we then should see
Love in its bright immortal purity.
Yet still we struggle in our earthly home
Until to us Love's perfect kingdom come.

The Epilogue.

"WELL," said the Host, "that is Love's
　　grotto, sure;
　A grotto such as we must oft endure
　The sight of, all made up of stucco
　　cells,
And spar, and plaister-casts, and oyster-shells.
You've pieced together broken scraps of love
Such as we see on earth.　In realms above,
Not here, love's perfect image we may find.
I have a wife; now, once I thought her kind,
And sweet, and loving, and, I know, was fair;
But, when we married, what a falling there
From all her winning ways; a thorough shrew.
Yes, love's ne'er perfect seen; too true, too true."

"Host," said the Knight, "'tis very true your life
Not always has been happy with your wife.
But think of those, whom we may often see,
Who happy live and lovingly agree,
And yet whose natures oft at variance are,
But they, with love, ward off the bickering jar.
And those who e'er harmoniously live
Increasing joy will to each other give.

E'en elder folks, too, we may sometimes see,
Whose life has been all love, around whose knee
Are children's children; they to all are kind,
And all will in love's warmest feeling bind.
Do not all these show love's majestic power,
That, e'en around us though earth's darkness lower
Our earthly selves war vainly 'gainst his might,
He shines on us, and brings, 'mid darkness, light?"

"Well," said the Miller, "I can't talk like you,
Sir Knight, but all that you have said is true.
For we old married men can pretty well
The average of love among us tell.
Some, like our Host, will grumble; more or less
All do the same, but all will marriage bless;
That is, 'mid their opinions strike the mean,
And then their general thought will soon be seen."

Then spake the Reeve. "All this is very well,
But there is no man can exactly tell.
He only knows—why, only what he knows,
And that's but little, though that often shows
More than he cares to know. Folks won't be wise,
Their weakness ever is to generalize,
And say, 'All men are this,' 'All women that,'
When they scarce know what 'tis they're aiming at.
Each knows some little, then, at Fancy's call,
Will talk as if he thought that he knew all."

Now set the sun, but gorgeous gold and red
Kept bright his memory after he had fled,

THE EPILOGUE.

As toward the glowing light the pale blue crept,
By the dark zenith to be overswept.
On sombre earth still strove the falling light,
Dying reluctantly ere lost in night,
Where dark with shadow was each lighter hue,
And deep tones faded, until lost to view
At little distance, where all things seemed one,
Where light scarce lived 'mid mystic shadow dun;
Some branch, some gate-post, might detain a ray
Of straggling light; our dresses, faces, they
Showed darkly, save when one turned, looking west,
And the half light would on his features rest.

The best of friends must part, the proverb says,
So, on the road of life, in various ways,
Each man must needs from pleasant friends retire,
As duty, pleasure, or stern fate require.
My fellow-mortals now began to say
'Twas time for them to take their homeward way,
'Twas late; and soon the laughter which attends
The leave-taking of many cheerful friends
Was heard, as hands were shaken all around,
Where good byes and fair wishes did abound.
When they were gone, I of the Host did ask
About a matter which has been a task
Oft to my puzzled brain. He answered me
Not clearly, so that I could plainly see
The same thing puzzled him, and, when again,
I pressed and asked him for an answer plain,

He said, "Put on your thinking-cap, and guess;
To this grave matter now your mind address."
Then drooped my head (as when this tale began)
Upon my breast, and through my mind there ran
Thoughts swift and varied, but I found no thread
Could draw reflections scattered to one head;
So, looking downward with half-closed eyes,
And half unto self speaking, "Pray, advise,
And help me in this matter, good Sir Host,
Or I, in this maze wandering, may be lost."
Still deep I pondered, and as no reply
Came from the courteous Host, I wondered why,
And raised my voice and eyes. He was not there,
Nor any other. Could it be, in air
They had dissolved? They all were out of sight,
Nor sound nor sign had heralded their flight.
One moment they were here; the next, were gone;
They'd vanished all. Again I was alone.
It was so strange. My wits I scarce believed,
Then thought that, possibly, I'd been deceived;
Perhaps 'twas so while they my fancy cheered,
But 'twas not so now they had disappeared,
For now I knew—ah! yes, I knew it all,
Whate'er it was, yet could not quite recall
To memory how all had come about,
Still in some hazy state of semi-doubt,
Certain of nothing but uncertainty,
Yet not quite certain if such thing might be.
At last, as mortal man on mortal earth,
I wondered what had given such fancies birth,

But quickly drove such wonder from my brain,
Lest I should start on such a chase again.

And now, at last, from you who, on the way,
Have ridden by my side this livelong day,
Kind Reader, I must part ; you're a true friend,
For you've kept by me, even to the end.
But here our roads diverge, for now in sight
Is the book's end ; yet, ere we take our flight,
I'll say, and hope I say it not in vain,
Good-bye, good-bye, and may we meet again.

LONDON
PRINTED BY GILBERT AND RIVINGTON, LIMITED,
ST. JOHN'S HOUSE, CLERKENWELL ROAD.

[D.—15.7.87.—V.]

A CATALOGUE OF BOOKS FOR THE YOUNG,

OF ALL AGES,

SUITABLE FOR PRESENTS AND SCHOOL PRIZES,

ARRANGED ACCORDING TO PRICES,

FROM HALF-A-GUINEA TO SIXPENCE EACH.

PUBLISHED BY

GRIFFITH, FARRAN, OKEDEN & WELSH

(SUCCESSORS TO NEWBERY AND HARRIS),

WEST CORNER OF ST. PAUL'S CHURCHYARD, LONDON.

E. P. DUTTON AND CO., NEW YORK.

A

BOOKS FOR THE YOUNG.

Arranged according to Prices.

7/6 — *Seven Shillings and Sixpence each, cloth elegant. Illustrated.*
Alice's Wonderland Birthday Book. By E. STANLEY LEATHES and C. E. W. HOLMES.
Child Elves. By M. G.
The Looking-Glass for the Mind. With Cuts by BEWICK. An Introduction by CHARLES WELSH.
Wanderings of a Beetle. By E. P. WARREN.

6/- — **KINGSTON'S SERIES OF SIX SHILLING BOOKS.**
Twelve Volumes. Each containing from 450 to 550 pages, well Illustrated by the best Artists. Imperial 16mo, cloth elegant, bevelled boards, gilt edges.
Hurricane Hurry.
Master of his Fate. By A. BLANCHE. Trans. by Rev. M. R. BARNARD.
Middy and Ensign. By G. MANVILLE FENN.
The Missing Ship; or, Notes from the Log of the *Ouzel Galley*.
Paddy Finn: The Adventures of an Irish Midshipman.
The Three Midshipmen.
The Three Lieutenants; or, Naval life in the Nineteenth Century.
The Three Commanders; or, Active Service Afloat in Modern Times.
The Three Admirals, and the Adventures of their Young Followers.
True Blue; or, a British Seaman of the Old School.
Will Weatherhelm; or, The Yarn of an Old Sailor.
Won from the Waves; or, The Story of Maiden May.
Young Buglers: A Tale of the Peninsular War. By G. A. HENTY.

6/- — *Six Shillings each, cloth elegant, with Illustrations.*
The Bird and Insects' Post Office. By R. BLOOMFIELD. (Or paper boards, price 3s. 6d.)
Flyaway Fairies and Baby Blossoms. By L. CLARKSON.
Golden Threads from an Ancient Loom. By LYDIA HANDS.
His Little Royal Highness. By RUTH OGDEN.
Journey to the Centre of the Earth. By JULES VERNE.
Little Loving Heart's Poem Book. By M. E. TUPPER.
Mabel in Rhymeland. By EDWARD HOLLAND, C.C.S.
Mamma's Bible Stories. 3 Vols., in cardboard box.
The Vanderbilts and the Story of their Fortune. By W. A. CROFFUT.

5/- — *Five Shillings each, cloth elegant. Illus. by eminent Artists.*
All Round the Clock. By H. M. BENNETT and R. E. MACK. 4to, Boards.
Belle's Pink Boots. By JOANNA H. MATTHEWS. Gilt edges.
The Day of Wonders. By M. SULLIVAN. Gilt edges.
Dethroned; A Story for Girls. By the Author of "Girlhood Days."
Extraordinary Nursery Rhymes; New, yet Old. Small 4to.

GRIFFITH, FARRAN, OKEDEN AND WELSH,

Five Shillings each—continued.

Favourite Picture Book (The) and Nursery Companion. Compiled anew by UNCLE CHARLIE. With 450 Illustrations by ABSOLON, ANELAY, BENNETT, BROWNE (PHIZ), SIR JOHN GILBERT, T. LANDSEER, LEECH, PROUT, HARRISON WEIR, and others. Medium 4to, cloth elegant (or coloured Illustrations, 10s. 6d.).

** This may also be had in Two Vols., cloth, price 3s., or coloured Illustrations, 5s.; also in Four parts, in paper boards, fancy wrapper, price 1s. each, or coloured Illustrations, 2s. each.

First Christmas. By HOFFMANN.
From May to Christmas at Thorne Hill. By Mrs. D. P. SANDFORD.
Gladys Ramsay. By Mrs. M. DOUGLAS. Crown 8vo.
Goody Two Shoes. In a Fac-simile Cover of the Original, with introduction by CHARLES WELSH.
Harris's Cabinet: { The Butterfly's Ball. | The Lion's Masquerade. The Elephant's Ball. | The Peacock at Home. } Or in Four Parts at 1s. each.
History of the Robins. By Mrs. TRIMMER. Small 4to, gilt edges.
Little Margit. By M. A. HOYER.
Little People of Asia. By OLIVE THORNE MILLER.
Merry Songs for Little Voices. Words by Mrs. BRODERIP. Music by THOMAS MURBY. Fcap. 4to.
Nothing Venture, Nothing Have. By ANNE BEALE.
Patrañas; or, SPANISH STORIES, LEGENDARY AND TRADITIONAL.
The Pattern Life. By W. CHATTERTON DIX.
Pictures and Songs for Little Children.
Queen of the Meadow. By R. E. MACK.
Queer Pets and their Doings. By the author of "Little People of Asia."
Wee Babies. By IDA WAUGH and AMY E. BLANCHARD.

Five Shilling Series of
TALES OF TRAVEL AND ADVENTURE.

Crown 8vo, well printed on good paper, and strongly bound in cloth elegant, bevelled boards, gilt edges. Each volume contains from 300 to 400 pages of solid reading. Fully illustrated by eminent Artists.

The Briny Deep. By CAPTAIN TOM.
From Cadet to Captain. By J. PERCY GROVES.
The Cruise of the Theseus. By ARTHUR KNIGHT.
The Duke's Own. By J. PERCY GROVES.
Friends though Divided. By GEO. A. HENTY.
Hair-breadth Escapes. By the Rev. H. C. ADAMS.
Masaniello. By F. BAYFORD HARRISON.
Mystery of Beechy Grange (The). By the Rev. H. C. ADAMS.
Perils in the Transvaal and Zululand. By the Rev. H. C. ADAMS.
Rival Crusoes (The). By W. H. G. KINGSTON.
A Search for the Mountain of Gold. By W. MURPHY.

BOOKS FOR THE YOUNG PUBLISHED BY

Five Shillings series—continued.

A Soldier Born. By J. PERCY GROVES.
In Times of Peril. By GEO. A. HENTY.
Who did it? or, HOLMWOOD PRIORY. By the Rev. H. C. ADAMS.
Who was Philip? By the Rev. H. C. ADAMS.

THE BOYS' OWN FAVOURITE LIBRARY.

3/6

Twenty-seven Volumes, price Three Shillings and Sixpence each.

Each volume contains from 300 to 450 pages of solid reading, well illustrated by the best Artists. Crown 8vo, cloth elegant, gilt edges.

Mark Seaworth. By W. H. G. KINGSTON.
Hurricane Hurry. By W. H. G. KINGSTON.
Salt Water. By W. H. G. KINGSTON.
Out on the Pampas. By G. A. HENTY.
Peter the Whaler. By W. H. G. KINGSTON.
The Three Admirals. By W. H. G. KINGSTON.
Early Start in Life. By E. MARRYAT NORRIS.
Fred Markham in Russia. By W. H. G. KINGSTON.
College Days at Oxford. By Rev. H. C. ADAMS.
The Young Francs-Tireurs. By G. A. HENTY.
The Three Midshipmen. By W. H. G. KINGSTON.
The Fiery Cross. By BARBARA HUTTON.
Our Soldiers. By W. H. G. KINGSTON.
The Three Commanders. By W. H. G. KINGSTON.
The Three Lieutenants. By W. H. G. KINGSTON.
Manco, The Peruvian Chief. By W. H. G. KINGSTON.
Our Sailors. By W. H. G. KINGSTON.
John Deane. By W. H. G. KINGSTON.
Travel, War, and Shipwreck. By Colonel PARKER GILLMORE.
Chums. By HARLEIGH SEVERNE.
African Wanderers. By Mrs. R. LEE.
Tales of the White Cockade. By BARBARA HUTTON.
The Missing Ship. By W. H. G. KINGSTON.
Will Weatherhelm. By W. H. G. KINGSTON.
True Blue. By W. H. G. KINGSTON.
The North Pole, and How CHARLIE WILSON discovered it.
Harty the Wanderer. By FARLEIGH OWEN.

THE GIRLS' OWN FAVOURITE LIBRARY.

3/6

Twenty-seven Volumes, price Three Shillings and Sixpence each.

Each volume contains from 300 to 400 pages of solid reading, well illustrated by the best Artists. Cr. 8vo, cloth elegant, gilt edges.

Guide, Philosopher, and Friend. By Mrs. HERBERT MARTIN.
Her Title of Honour. By HOLME LEE.
Michaelmas Daisy. By SARAH DOUDNEY.
The New Girl. By Mrs. GELLIE.
The Oak Staircase. By M. and C. LEE.

GRIFFITH, FARRAN, OKEDEN AND WELSH,

The Girls' Own Favourite Library.
Three Shillings and Sixpence each—continued. 3/6

For a Dream's Sake. By Mrs. HERBERT MARTIN.
My Mother's Diamonds. By MARIA J. GREEB.
My Sister's Keeper. By LAURA M. LANE.
Shiloh. By W. M. L. JAY.
Holden with the Cords. By W. M. L. JAY.
"Bonnie Lesley." By Mrs. HERBERT MARTIN.
Left Alone. By FRANCIS CARR.
Very Genteel. By the Author of "Mrs. Jerningham's Journal."
Gladys the Reaper. By ANNE BEALE.
Stephen the Schoolmaster. By Mrs. GELLIE (M. E. B.).
Isabel's Difficulties. By M. R. CAREY.
Court and Cottage. By Mrs. EMMA MARSHALL.
Rosamond Fane. By M. and C. LEE.
Simplicity and Fascination. By ANNE BEALE.
Millicent and Her Cousins. By the Hon. A. BETHELL.
Aunt Hetty's Will. By M. M. POLLARD.
Silver Linings. By Mrs. BRAY.
Theodora. By EMILIA MARRYAT NORRIS.
Alda Graham. By EMILIA MARRYAT NORRIS.
A Wayside Posy. By FANNY LABLACHE.
Through a Refiner's Fire. By ELEANOR HOLMES.
A Generous Friendship; or, THE HAPPENINGS OF A NEW ENGLAND SUMMER.
A Country Mouse. By Mrs. HERBERT MARTIN.

Price Three Shillings and Sixpence each. 3/6
Elegantly bound, and illustrated by the best Authors.

Bird and Insects' Post Office (The). By ROBERT BLOOMFIELD. Crown 4to, paper boards, with Chromo side (or cloth elegant, 6s.)
Bunch of Berries (A), AND THE DIVERSIONS THEREOF. By LEADER SCOTT.
Castles and their Heroes. By BARBARA HUTTON.
Child Pictures from Dickens. Illustrated.
Clement's Trial and Victory. By M. E. B. (Mrs. GELLIE).
Daisy Days; a Colour Book for Children. By Mrs. A. M. CLAUSEN.
Every-day Life in Our Public Schools. By CHAS. EYRE PASCOE.
In Time of War. By JAS. F. COBB.
Joachim's Spectacles. By M. and C. LEE.
Lee (Mrs.) Anecdotes of the Habits and Instincts of Animals.
　,, Anecdotes of the Habits and Instincts of Birds, Reptiles, and Fishes.
　,, Adventures in Australia.
Lily and Her Brothers. By C. E. L.
Little Chicks and Baby Tricks. By IDA WAUGH.
Little May's Friend. By ANNIE WHITTEM.
The Little Wonderbox. By JEAN INGELOW. A series of Six Vols.

ST. PAUL'S CHURCHYARD, LONDON.

BOOKS FOR THE YOUNG PUBLISHED BY

3/6

Three Shillings and Sixpence each—continued.

My Friend and My Enemy. By PAUL BLAKE.
Nimpo's Troubles. By OLIVE THORNE MILLER.
Old Corner Annual for 1888. Illustrated.
Perils of the Pacific; a Tale of the Sea. By ROBERT BROWN.
Reached at Last. By R. H. CUTTER.
Restful Work for Youthful Hands. By S. F. A. CAULFIELD.
Sermons for Children. By A. DE COPPET.
Talks about Plants. By Mrs. LANKESTER.
Two Stories of Two. By STELLA AUSTIN.
Under the Mistletoe. By LIZZIE LAWSON and R. E. MACK. 4to, boards.
Unwelcome Guest. By ESME STUART.

2/6

THE "BUNCHY" SERIES OF HALF-CROWN BOOKS.

Crown 8vo. Cloth elegant, bevelled boards, gilt edges, fully Illustrated by the best Artists.

African Pets. By F. CLINTON PARRY.
Bunchy. By E. C. PHILLIPS.
Bryan and Katie. By ANNETTE LYSTER.
Cast Adrift: the Story of a Waif. By Mrs. H. H. MARTIN.
Daring Voyage across the Atlantic. By the Brothers ANDREWS.
Dolly, Dear! By MARY E. GELLIE.
Every Inch a King. By Mrs. J. WORTHINGTON BLISS.
Family Feats. By Mrs. R. M. BRAY.
Fearless Frank. By MARY E. GELLIE.
A Gem of an Aunt. By Mrs. GELLIE (M. E. B.)
Gerty and May. By the Author of "Our White Violet."
Grandfather. By E. C. PHILLIPS, Author of "Bunchy."
Great and Small. By Miss HARRIET POOLE.
Growing Up. By JENNETT HUMPHREYS.
Hilda and Her Doll. By E. C. PHILLIPS.
House on the Bridge. By C. E. BOWEN.
Hugh's Sacrifice. By CECIL MARRYAT NORRIS.
Mischievous Jack. By C. E. L.
Nora's Trust. By Mrs. GELLIE (M. E. B.).
Our Aubrey. By E. C. PHILLIPS.
Punch. By E. C. PHILLIPS.
St. Aubyn's Laddie. By E. C. PHILLIPS.
Ten of Them. By Mrs. R. M. BRAY.
"Those Unlucky Twins!" By ANNETTE LYSTER.
Two Rose Trees. By Mrs. MINNIE DOUGLAS.
The Venturesome Twins. By Mrs. GELLIE. Crown 8vo.
Ways and Tricks of Animals. By MARY HOOPER.
We Four. By Mrs. R. M. BRAY.

GRIFFITH, FARRAN, OKEDEN AND WELSH,

Two Shillings and Sixpence each—continued.

Boy Slave in Bokhara. By DAVID KER.
Boy's Own Toy Maker (The): A Practical Illustrated Guide to the useful employment of Leisure Hours. By E. LANDELLS.
Choice Extracts from the Standard Authors. By the Editor of "Poetry for the Young." 3 vols. (2s. 6d. each.)
Cruise of Ulysses and His Men (The); or, Tales and Adventures from the Odyssey, for Boys and Girls. By C. M. BELL.
Girl's Own Toy Maker (The), AND BOOK OF RECREATION. By E. and A. LANDELLS. With 200 Illustrations.
Goody Two Shoes. A Reprint of the Original Edition, with Introduction by CHAS. WELSH.
Holly Berries. By AMY E. BLANCHARD. Coloured Illustrations by IDA WAUGH. 4to boards.
Ice Maiden AND OTHER STORIES. By HANS CHRISTIAN ANDERSEN.
Lesson Notes. By STAFFORD C. NORTHCOTE.
Little Child's Fable Book. Arranged Progressively in One, Two, and Three Syllables. 16 Pages, Illustrated. *Cheap Edition.*
Little Gipsy. By ELIE SAUVAGE. *Cheaper Edition.*
Little Pilgrim (The). Illustrated by HELEN PETRIE.
Model Yachts, and Model Yacht Sailing: HOW TO BUILD, RIG AND SAIL A SELF-ACTING MODEL YACHT. By JAS. E. WALTON, V.M.Y.C. Fcap. 4to, with 58 Woodcuts.
My Own Dolly. By AMY BLANCHARD and IDA WAUGH.
On the Leads. By Mrs. A. A. STRANGE BUTSON.
Sea and Sky. By J. R. BLAKISTON, M.A. Suitable for young people. Profusely Illustrated, and contains a Coloured Atlas of the Phenomena of Sea and Sky.
Science in the Nursery; or, Children's Toys. By T. W. ERLE.
Wild Horseman of the Pampas. By DAVID KER.

Two Shillings and Sixpence, cloth elegant, with Illustrations by Harrison Weir and other Eminent Artists.

As Yankees see us. By LEANDER RICHARDSON.
Animals and their Social Powers. By MARY TURNER-ANDREWES.
A Week by Themselves. By EMILIA MARRYAT NORRIS.
Babies' Crawling Rugs, and How to Make them. By EMMA S. WINDSOR.
Christmas Box.
Christmas Roses. By LIZZIE LAWSON and R. E. MACK. 4to, boards.
Christmas Tree Fairy. By R. E. MACK and Mrs. L. MACK.
Cleopatra.
Funny Fables for Little Folks.

BOOKS FOR THE YOUNG PUBLISHED BY

2/6

Two Shillings and Sixpence each—continued.

Granny's Story Box. With 20 Engravings.
Jack Frost and Betty Snow; Tales for Wintry Nights and Rainy Days.
London Cries. By LUKE LIMNER.
Madelon. By ESTHER CARR.
Margaret Kent. An American Story.
Odd Stories about Animals: told in Short and Easy Words.
Percy Pomo; or, the Autobiography of a South Sea Islander.
Secret of Wrexford (The). By ESTHER CARR.
Snowed Up. By EMILIA MARRYAT NORRIS.
Tales from Catland. Dedicated to the Young Kittens of England.
Talking Bird (The). By M. and E. KIRBY.
Three Nights. By CECIL MARRYAT NORRIS.
Tiny Stories for Tiny Readers in Tiny Words.
Trottie's Story Book: True Tales in Short Words and Large Type.
Tuppy; or, THE AUTOBIOGRAPHY OF A DONKEY.
Wandering Blindfold; or, A BOY'S TROUBLES. By MARY ALBERT.

NEW ILLUSTRATED QUARTO GIFT BOOKS.

Wreck of Hesperus. By H. W. Longfellow. Small quarto, cloth bevelled, stamped in gold and colour.

Uniform with the above.

The Village Blacksmith. | Keble's Evening Hymn.
The Sweet By-and-Bye.

COMICAL PICTURE BOOKS.

2/6

Two Shillings and Sixpence each, fancy boards.

Adventures of the Pig Family, The. By ARTHUR S. GIBSON. Sixteen pages Illustrations, oblong 4to, boards.
The March Hares and their friends. Uniform with the above. By the same author.

The following have Coloured Plates.

English Struwwelpeter (The): or PRETTY STORIES AND FUNNY PICTURES FOR LITTLE CHILDREN. After the celebrated German Work of Dr. HEINRICH HOFFMANN. Thirtieth Edition. Twenty-four pages of Illustrations (or mounted on linen, 5s.).
The Fools' Paradise. Mirth and Fun for Old and Young.
Funny Picture Book (The); or, 25 FUNNY LITTLE LESSONS. A free Translation from the German of "DER KLEINE ABC SCHÜTZE."
In the Land of Nod; a Fancy Story. By A. C. MARZATH.
Loves of Tom Tucker and Little Bo-Peep. Written and Illustrated by THOMAS HOOD.
Spectropia; or, SURPRISING SPECTRAL ILLUSIONS, showing Ghosts everywhere, and of any colour. By J. H. BROWN.

GRIFFITH, FARRAN, OKEDEN AND WELSH,

THE HOLIDAY LIBRARY.

A Series of 15 Volumes for Boys and Girls, well illustrated, and bound in cloth, with elegant design printed in gold and colours, gilt edges. The size is Foolscap 8vo, and as each volume contains upwards of 300 pages of interesting tales of all descriptions, they form one of the most attractive and saleable series in the market.

Price Two Shillings, each volume containing Two Tales, well Illustrated. 2/-

LIST OF BOOKS IN THE SERIES.

Vol.		Vol.	
I.	Sunny Days. / Wrecked, Not Lost.	VIII.	Children's Picnic. / Holiday Tales.
II.	Discontented Children. / Holidays among Mountains.	IX.	Christian Elliott. / Stolen Cherries.
III.	Adrift on the Sea. / Hofer the Tyrolese.	X.	Harry at School. / Claudine.
IV.	Alice and Beatrice. / Julia Maitland.	XI.	Our White Violet. / Fickle Flora.
V.	Among the Brigands. / Hero of Brittany.	XII.	William Tell. / Paul Howard's Captivity.
VI.	Cat and Dog. / Johnny Miller.	XIII.	Amy's Wish. / New Baby.
VII.	Children of the Parsonage. / Grandmamma's Relics.	XIV.	Neptune. / Crib and Fly.
		XV.	What became of Tommy / Geoffrey's Great Fault.

Two Shillings, cloth elegant, Illustrated.

Captain Fortescue's Handful. By C. MARRYATT NORRIS.
Children's Gallery. Four Parts, price 2s. each.
Elsie Dinsmore }
Elsie's Girlhood } By MARTHA FARQUHARSON.
Elsie's Holidays }
A Far-away Cousin. By K. D. CORNISH.
How to Make Dolls' Furniture AND TO FURNISH A DOLL'S HOUSE. With 70 Illustrations. Small 4to.
Illustrated Paper Model Maker. By E. LANDELLS. In envelope.
Mademoiselle's Story. By MADAME RYFFEL.
Mamma's Bible Stories. First Series. FOR HER LITTLE BOYS AND GIRLS.
Mamma's Bible Stories. Second Series.
Mamma's Bible Stories. Third Series. Illustrated by STANLEY BERKELEY. The three Volumes can be had in a handsome case. Price 6s.
Scenes of Animal Life and Character. FROM NATURE AND RECOLLECTION. In Twenty Plates. By J. B. 4to, fancy boards.
Seeking His Fortune. Uniform in size and price with above.
Two and Two; OR, FRENCH AND ENGLISH. By Mrs. SEYMOUR.
Wonders of Home, in Eleven Stories (The). By GRANDFATHER GREY.
Young Vocalist (The). Cloth boards. (Or paper, 1s.)

Price One Shilling and Sixpence each.

Babies' Museum (The). By UNCLE CHARLIE. Paper boards.

Children's Daily Help. By E. G. Bevelled boards, gilt edges.

Directory of Girls' Societies, Clubs, and Unions. Conducted on unprofessional principles. By S. F. A. CAULFIELD.

Little Margaret's Ride to the Isle of Wight; or, THE WONDERFUL ROCKING-HORSE. By Mrs. F. BROWN. Coloured Illustrations.

Our Wild Swan and other Pets. By HELEN WEBLEY PARRY, Author of "An Epitome of Anglican Church History." With coloured illustrations by HARRISON WEIR. Price 1s. 6d.

Rivals of the Cornfield. By the Author of "Geneviève's Story."

Seasons' Songs and Sketches. 4 Vols. small quarto. Price 1/6 each.
I. Spring. II. Summer. III. Autumn. IV. Winter.

Taking Tales. In Plain Language and large Type. Four vols. May also be had in 2 vols., 3s. 6d. each; and in 21 parts, cl. limp, price 6d. each.

ANGELO SERIES OF EIGHTEENPENNY BOOKS.

Square 16mo. Cloth elegant, fully Illustrated.

Angelo; or, THE PINE FOREST IN THE ALPS. By GERALDINE E. JEWSBURY. 5th Thousand.

Aunt Annette's Stories to Ada. By ANNETTE A. SALAMAN.

Brave Nelly; or, WEAK HANDS AND A WILLING HEART. By M. E. B. (Mrs. GELLIE). 5th Thousand.

Featherland; or, HOW THE BIRDS LIVED AT GREENLAWN. By G. M. FENN. 4th Thousand.

Humble Life: A Tale of HUMBLE HOMES. By the Author of "Gerty and May," &c.

Kingston's (W. H. G.) Child of the Wreck; or, THE LOSS OF THE ROYAL GEORGE.

Lee's (Mrs. R.) Playing at Settlers; or, THE FAGOT HOUSE.
——— Twelve Stories of the Sayings and Doings of Animals.

Little Lisette, THE ORPHAN OF ALSACE. By M. E. B. (Mrs. GELLIE).

Live Toys; or, ANECDOTES OF OUR FOUR-LEGGED AND OTHER PETS. By EMMA DAVENPORT.

Long Evenings; or, STORIES FOR MY LITTLE FRIENDS. By EMILIA MARRYAT.

Three Wishes (The). By Mrs. GELLIE (M. E. B.).

The CHERRY SERIES of EIGHTEENPENNY BOOKS. 1/6
PRESENTS AND PRIZES FOR BOYS AND GIRLS.

Thirty-six volumes, well illustrated, small 8vo, clearly printed on good paper, and strongly bound in elegant cloth boards, gilt edges.

Adventures in Fanti-land. By Mrs. R. LEE.
African Cruiser (The). By S. WHITCHURCH SADLER.
Always Happy; or, Anecdotes of Felix and his Sister.
Aunt Mary's Bran Pie. By the Author of "St. Olave's."
Battle and Victory. By C. E. BOWEN.
A Child's Influence. By LISA LOCKYER.
Constance and Nellie. By EMMA DAVENPORT.
Corner Cottage, and its Inmates. By FRANCES OSBORNE.
Distant Homes. By Mrs. J. E. AYLMER.
Father Time's Story Book. By KATHLEEN KNOX.
From Peasant to Prince. By Mrs. PIETZKER.
Girlhood Days. By Mrs. SEYMOUR.
Good in Everything. By Mrs. BARWELL.
Granny's Wonderful Chair. By B. F. BROWNE.
Happy Holidays. By EMMA DAVENPORT.
Happy Home. By LADY LUSHINGTON.
The Heroic Wife. By W. H. G. KINGSTON.
Helen in Switzerland. By LADY LUSHINGTON.
Holidays Abroad; or, Right at Last. By EMMA DAVENPORT.
Lucy's Campaign. By M. and C. LEE.
Lost in the Jungle. By AUGUSTA MARRYAT.
Louisa Broadhurst. By A. MILNER.
Master Bobby.
Mudge and Her Chicks.
My Grandmother's Budget. By Mrs. BRODERIP.
Our Birthdays. By EMMA DAVENPORT.
Our Home in the Marshland. By E. L. F.
Parted. By N. D'ANVERS.
Pictures of Girl Life. By C. A. HOWELL.
School Days in Paris. By M. S. JEUNE.
Starlight Stories. By FANNY LABLACHE.
Sunnyland Stories. By the Author of "St. Olave's."
Talent and Tatters.
Tittle-Tattle: and other Stories for Children.
Vicar of Wakefield (The).
Willie's Victory.

BOOKS FOR THE YOUNG PUBLISHED BY

1/-

THE HAWTHORN SERIES OF SHILLING BOOKS.
PRESENTS AND PRIZES FOR BOYS AND GIRLS.

Forty-two volumes, well illustrated, small 8vo, clearly printed on good paper, and strongly bound in elegant cloth boards.

Adrift on the Sea. By E. M. NORRIS.
Alice and Beatrice. By GRANDMAMMA.
Among the Brigands. By C. E. BOWEN.
Amy's Wish: A Fairy Tale. By Mr. G. TYLER.
Cat and Dog; or, Puss and the Captain.
Children of the Parsonage. By the Author of "Gerty and May."
Children's Picnic (The). By E. MARRYAT NORRIS.
Christian Elliott; or, Mrs. Danver's Prize. By L. N. COMYN.
Claudine; or, Humility the Basis of all the Virtues.
Crib and Fly: the Story of Two Terriers.
Daughter of a Genius (The). By Mrs. HOFLAND.
Discontented Children (The). By M. and E. KIRBY.
Ellen, the Teacher. By Mrs. HOFLAND.
Eskdale Herd Boy (The). By LADY STODDART.
Fickle Flora and her Seaside Friends. By EMMA DAVENPORT.
Geoffrey's Great Fault. By E. MARRYAT NORRIS.
Grandmamma's Relics. By C. E. BOWEN.
Harry at School. A Story for Boys. By E. MARRYAT NORRIS.
Hero of Brittany (The); or, The Story of Bertrand du Guesclin.
History of the Robins (The). By Mrs. TRIMMER.
Hofer, the Tyrolese. By the Author of "William Tell."
Holiday Tales. By FLORENCE WILFORD.
Holidays among the Mountains. By M. BETHAM EDWARDS.
Johnny Miller. By FELIX WEISS.
Julia Maitland. By M. and E. KIRBY.
Life and Perambulations of a Mouse (The).
Memoir of Bob, the Spotted Terrier.
Mrs. Leicester's School. By CHARLES and MARY LAMB.
Neptune: The Autobiography of a Newfoundland Dog.
Never Wrong; or, The Young Disputant; and It was only in Fun.
New Baby (The). By the Author of "Our White Violet."
Our White Violet. By the Author of "Gerty and May."
Paul Howard's Captivity. By E. MARRYAT NORRIS.
Right and Wrong. By the Author of "Always Happy."
Scottish Orphans (The). By LADY STODDART.
Son of a Genius (The). By Mrs. HOFLAND.
Stolen Cherries (The); or Tell the Truth at once.
Sunny Days. By the Author of "Our White Violet."
Theodore; or the Crusaders. By Mrs. HOFLAND.
What became of Tommy. By E. MARRYAT NORRIS.
William Tell, the Patriot of Switzerland. By FLORIAN.
Wrecked, not Lost. By the Hon. Mrs. DUNDAS.

GRIFFITH, FARRAN, OKEDEN AND WELSH,

Price One Shilling each—continued.   1/-

Easy Reading for Little Readers. Paper Boards.
Fragments of Knowledge for Little Folk. Paper Boards.
The Nursery Companion. Paper Boards.
The Picturesque Primer. Paper Boards.
<small>These Four Volumes contain about 450 pictures; each one being complete in itself, and bound in an attractive paper cover, in boards (also with coloured Illustrations, 2s.)
The Four Volumes bound together form the "Favourite Picture Book," bound in cloth, price 5s., or coloured Illustrations, gilt edges, 10s. 6d.</small>

The Butterfly's Ball (reproduced). With an Introduction by CHAS.
The Elephant's Ball. Ditto.   [WELSH.
The Lion's Masquerade. Ditto.
The Peacock at Home. Ditto.

The Child's Duty.	Meta in England.
Cock Robin. Sewed.	Mr. Fox's Pinch for Pride.
Courtship of Jenny Wren. Sewed.	Three Fairy Tales. By PAN.
Fairy Folk. By E. LACKY.	Whittington and his Cat.
Goody Two Shoes. Cloth.	The Wreck.
House that Jack Built. Sewed.	Young Communicant's Manual.

Babies' Museum (The): OR, RHYMES, JINGLES, AND DITTIES FOR THE NURSERY. By UNCLE CHARLIE. Fully Illustrated. (Or paper boards, 1s. 6d.)
Bible Lilies. Scripture Selections for Morning and Evening.
Cowslip (The). Fully Illustrated cloth, 1s. *plain.*
Daisy (The). Fully Illustrated cloth, 1s. *plain.*
Dame Partlett's Farm. AN ACCOUNT OF THE RICHES SHE OBTAINED BY INDUSTRY, &c. Coloured Illustrations, sewed.
Fairy Folk. By E. LECKY.
Fairy Gifts: OR, A WALLET OF WONDERS. By KATHLEEN KNOX. Illustrated by KATE GREENAWAY. Fancy boards.
Fairy Land. By the late THOMAS AND JANE HOOD. Fancy boards.
Female Christian Names, AND THEIR TEACHINGS. A Gift Book for Girls. By MARY E. BROMFIELD. Gilt edges.
Flowers of Grace. Scripture Selections for every day.
Hand Shadows, to be thrown upon the Wall. Novel and amusing figures formed by the hand. By HENRY BURSILL. Two Series in one. (Or coloured Illustrations, 1s. 6d.)
Lufness. A Sequel to the Wreck. By ETHEL.
Nine Lives of a Cat (The): a Tale of Wonder. Written and Illustrated by C. H. BENNETT. 24 Coloured Engravings, sewed.
Peter Piper. PRACTICAL PRINCIPLES OF PLAIN AND PERFECT PRONUNCIATION. Coloured Illustrations, sewed.
Primrose Pilgrimage (The): a Woodland Story. By M. BETHAM EDWARDS. Illustrated by MACQUOID. Sewed.
Rhymes and Pictures ABOUT BREAD, TEA, SUGAR, COTTON, COALS, AND GOLD. By WILLIAM NEWMAN. Seventy-two Illustrations. Price 1s. plain; 2s. 6d. coloured.
Rosebuds and Promises. A Little Book of Scripture Texts.

14   BOOKS FOR THE YOUNG PUBLISHED BY

1/-

One Shilling each—continued.

Short and Simple Prayers, with Hymns for the Use of Children. By the Author of "Mamma's Bible Stories." Cloth.

Short Stories for Children about Animals. In Words of One Syllable. Fully Illustrated by HARRISON WEIR.

Christmas Carols. For Children in Church, at Home, and in School. Words by Mrs. HERNAMAN, and Music by ALFRED REDHEAD. Twenty-two Carols. Price 1½d. each; or complete in paper cover, price 1s. 6d. each in Two Volumes; or in One Vol., cloth, price 3s. 6d. The Words only, price 1d. for each Series. List of the Carols :—

1. Jesus in the Manger.
2. The Birthday of Birthdays.
3. The Welcome Home.
4. Carol to Jesus Sleeping.
5. The Lambs in the Field.
6. Carol for the Children of Jesus.
7. Christmas Songs.
8. Round about the Christmas Tree.
9. Old Father Christmas.
10. We'll Gather round the Fire.
11. Carol we high.
12. The Prince of Peace.
13. Carol for Christmas Eve.
14. The Babe of Bethlehem.
15. The King in the Stable.
16. The Infant Jesus.
17. The Holy Innocents.
18. Epiphany.
19. A Merry Christmas.
20. The Christmas Party.
21. Light and Love.
22. The Christmas Stocking.

Upside Down; or, TURNOVER TRAITS. By THOMAS HOOD.

Whittington and his Cat. Coloured Illustrations, sewed.

Wreck. By ETHEL.

Young Vocalist (The). A Collection of Twelve Songs, each with an Accompaniment for the Pianoforte. By Mrs. MOUNSEY BARTHOLOMEW. (Or bound in cloth, price 2s.)

9d.

Price 9d. each, elegantly bound in Paper Boards, with Covers in Chromo-lithography.

THE TINY NATURAL HISTORY SERIES

OF STORY BOOKS ABOUT ANIMALS FOR LITTLE READERS.

ALL PROFUSELY ILLUSTRATED BY THE BEST ARTISTS.

Especially adapted for School Prizes and Rewards. In one way or another, the books either impart knowledge about Animals, or inculcate the desirableness of treating them with kindness.

Little Nellie's Bird Cage. By Mrs. R. LEE, Author of "The African Wanderers," &c.

The Tiny Menagerie. By Mrs. R. LEE, Author of "The African Wanderers," &c.

The Dog Postman. By the Author of "Odd Stories."

The Mischievous Monkey. By the Author of "Odd Stories."

Lily's Letters from the Farm. By MARY HOOPER, Author of "Ways and Tricks of Animals."

Our Dog Prin. By MARY HOOPER, Author of "Ways and Tricks of Animals."

Little Neddie's Menagerie. By Mrs. R. LEE, Author of "The African Wanderers," &c.

Frolicsome Frisk and his Friends. By the Author of "Trottie's Story Book."

Wise Birds and Clever Dogs. By the Author of "Tuppy," "Tiny Stories," &c.

Artful Pussy. By the Author of "Odd Stories," &c.

The Pet Pony. By the Author of "Trottie's Story Book."

Bow Wow Bobby. By the Author of "Tuppy," "Odd Stories," &c.

The above 12 vols. in Cardboard Box with Picture Top, price 9s.

Only a Kitten. By MAUD RANDALL.

GRIFFITH, FARRAN, OKEDEN AND WELSH,

In 21 Parts, cloth limp, fancy binding, with Chromo on side.
Price 6d. each.   **6d.**

TAKING TALES FOR COTTAGE HOMES.
Fully illustrated.
N.B.—Each Tale is Illustrated and complete in itself.

1. The Miller of Hillbrook: A RURAL TALE.
2. Tom Trueman: A SAILOR IN A MERCHANTMAN.
3. Michael Hale and His Family in Canada.
4. John Armstrong, THE SOLDIER.
5. Joseph Rudge, THE AUSTRALIAN SHEPHERD.
6. Life Underground; OR, DICK THE COLLIERY BOY.
7. Life on the Coast; OR, THE LITTLE FISHER GIRL.
8. Adventures of Two Orphans in London.
9. Early Days on Board a Man-of-War.
10. Walter, the Foundling: A TALE OF OLDEN TIMES.
11. The Tenants of Sunnyside Farm.
12. Holmwood; OR, THE NEW ZEALAND SETTLER.
13. A Bit of Fun, and what it cost.
14. Sweethearts: A TALE OF VILLAGE LIFE.
15. Helpful Sam. By M. A. B.
16. Little Pretty. By F. BAYFORD HARRISON.
17. A Wise Woman. By F. BAYFORD HARRISON.
18. Saturday Night. By F. BAYFORD HARRISON.
19. Second Best. By F. BAYFORD HARRISON.
20. Little Betsy. By Mrs. E. RELTON.
21. Louie White's Hop-picking. By Miss JENNER.

N.B.—The first Twelve parts may also be had in 4 volumes, 1s. 6d. each vol., and 2 volumes, 3s. 6d. each vol.

THE PRIZE STORY BOOK SERIES.
A Series of Six elegant little books for children from five to seven years of age, price 6d. each.

2. The Sand Cave.
1. The Picnic.
3. So-Fat and Mew-Mew at Home.
4. So-Fat and Mew-Mew away from Home.
5. The Birthday.
6. The Robins.

THE CHRISTMAS STOCKING SERIES.
A new Illustrated Series of Gift Books, with coloured cover and ... Frontispiece. Six volumes, price 6d. each.

The Christmas Stocking.
From Santa Claus.
Under the Christmas Tree.
Kitty Clover.
Robin Redbreast.
Twinkle-Twinkle.

ST. PAUL'S CHURCHYARD, LONDON.

BOOKS FOR THE YOUNG PUBLISHED BY

6d.

OUR BOYS' LITTLE LIBRARY.
PICTURES AND READING FOR LITTLE FOLK.

A Series of Twelve elegant little volumes in Cloth extra, with Picture on front, price 6d. each. The 12 vols. in a Box, price 6s. Every page is Illustrated.

They are especially suited for School Prizes and Rewards.

1. Papa's Pretty Gift Book.
2. Mamma's Pretty Gift Book.
3. Neddy's Picture Story Book.
4. Stories for Play Time.
5. The Christmas Gift Book.
6. The Prize Picture Book.
7. Little Tommy's Story Book.
8. Bright Picture Pages.
9. My Little Boy's Story Book.
10. What Santa Claus gave me.
11. Tiny Stories for Tiny Boys.
12. Little Boy Blue's Picture Book.

OUR GIRLS' LITTLE LIBRARY.
PICTURES AND READING FOR LITTLE FOLK.

A Series of Twelve elegant little volumes in Cloth, with Picture on front, price 6d. each. The 12 vols. in Box, price 6s. Every page is Illustrated.

They are especially suited for School Prizes and Rewards.

1. Nellie's Picture Stories.
2. Stories and Pictures for Little Troublesome.
3. Little Trotabout's Picture Stories.
4. Birdie's Scrap Book.
5. Stories for Little Curly Locks.
6. Bright Pictures for Roguish Eyes.
7. Daisy's Picture Album.
8. Wee-Wee Stories for Wee-Wee Girls.
9. May's Little Story Book.
10. Gipsy's Favourite Companion.
11. My Own Story Book.
12. Pretty Pet's Gift Book.

THE HOLLY SERIES OF SIXPENNY TOY BOOKS.

With original designs by IDA WAUGH. Exquisitely printed in bright colours, and issued in attractive and elegant covers. Verses by AMY BLANCHARD. Price 6d. each.

The following is a List of the Books in the Series.

1. Holly Gatherers.
2. Little May.
3. Horatio Hamilton Harris.
4. Our Boys.
5. The Christmas Carol.
6. Our Pussy Cat.

Ah Chin-Chin; HIS VOYAGE AND ADVENTURES. By F. CARRUTHERS GOULD.

4d.

THE BLUE BELL SERIES.

A new Illustrated Series of Beautiful Gift Books, containing numerous Pictures and Coloured Plates in each. Six vols., price 4d. each.

Little Blue Bell.
Oranges and Lemons.
May-time and Play-time.
Sweet as Honey.
Good as Gold.
Summer Days and Winter Ways.

OUR FATHER'S GIFTS.

A Series of Four beautiful little Books of Scripture Texts for one month. Illustrated, 48mo size, 4 Vols. 4d. each.

His Loving-kindnesses.
His Good Promises.
His Testimonies.
His Covenants.

GRIFFITH, FARRAN, OKEDEN AND WELSH.

www.ingramcontent.com/pod-product-compliance
Lightning Source LLC
Chambersburg PA
CBHW030257170426
43202CB00009B/779